ADVANCED CHESS MODEL III-THE SYNERGISTICS INFORMATICS OF THE QUADRUPLE SET GAME,

BOOK 4 VOL. 1 GAME # 1, (Q.4.1 G1), (G-G)/(G-G)/(A-A)/(A-A)

The Quadruple Set Game

SIAFA B. NEAL

Advanced Chess- Model III, The Synergistics Informatics of The Quadruple Set Game,
Book 4 Vol. 1 Game # 1, (Q.4.1 G1), (G-G)/(G-G)/(A-A)/(A-A)
Copyright © 2025 by Siafa B. Neal

Printed in the United States of America.

ISBN
979-8-89633-017-2 (Paperback)
979-8-89633-018-9 (eBook)

Page Solutions – Bluegrass Bound Books
541 Buttermilk Pike
Crescent Springs, KY 41017

Genre: Non-fiction, Young Adult, Juvenile, Educational, Instructional

SALUTATIONS

Attention all Toy Manufactures, Computer Science Engineers (Silicon Valley) and Investors (Business Model Planners).

Message: Both the hardware prototype and the applications software (electronic applications for gaming) of this new dynamic game may generate tremendous rewards beyond one's wildest imagination. This space-age game will indeed be new on the market and holds tremendous potentials and promises. It is my hope, that one day, the classic of this game of which classic gamers would as a collector's item, may generate interest into an Olympic Sport, whereby, both humans and robots alike compete for the World Championship series.

With this concept in mind, I extend my sincere greeting and salutations to all groups to whom this message concerns. It is likely, perhaps, that one day soon, this game may be the centerpiece of one of the recreational activities on the Martian colonies of the planet Mars and may be played for extended hours on end by Astronauts and Martian colonies alike.

May the Forces of Goodness be with you! Do feel free to pass this message onwards to friends pending for patent and should be on the market in a short while. Your Comments and Reviews are always Welcomed! (https://www.amazon.com/author/siafabneal).

Enjoy and Have Fun.

Sincerely,
Siafa B. Neal

Contact Information:
Author/Inventor Siafa B. Neal
Address: 1212 Iron Horse Circle, Colton, CA 92324
Email: chessplayer3334@gmail.com

TABLE OF CONTENTS

MESSAGE FROM GRAND MASTER SIAFA B. NEAL

The discovery of the 3-D Chess World, with the power of innovative creativity, our inspiration has always been and still is you. We fell in love with the game of chess repeatedly. It is no secret that the high-concept book of Advanced 3-D Chess craze is now sweeping the continental United States, Europe, and Asia.

The board game of the Longitudinal Star Gate 14 Model, Model III, which represents a quantum leap in design, innovation, and state-of-the-art engineering, delivers hours of fun and entertainment for seasoned players. This game receives a great deal of well-deserved hype. Besides the mind-blowing, mind-baffling, and overwhelming concepts of Advanced Chess which the model offers to chess enthusiasts worldwide, the board game offers an avenue whereby Advance thinkers may demonstrate their intellectual capabilities. The board game which is now becoming ubiquitous and famous for providing chess players who crave for hours of entertainment and for opportunities to divulge into the pseudo-dynamic and quasi-kinetic World of Advanced Chess to evaluate their spectral Logistics aptitude for Diagnostic and Prognostic intelligence analysis. This is the juncture where the old concepts meet the new concepts of chess playing indulgence. Be a participant in making history by making your purchase of this book and the game boards. (https://www.amazon.com/author/siafabneal).

Advanced 3-D Chess is clearly a better way for intellectual stimulation. Increasingly today's gamers are looking for immersive experiences that bring them right to the heart of unique gaming opportunities and challenges. This explains a great deal about the growth of the gaming industry and the demand for Advance 3-D Chess, Inc. business experiences, books, and products. Our new game model is unparalleled and unrivaled both in design and innovation. We achieve the distinction of being the most innovative and unique in chess modeling designs and continue to advance and to promote unique, one-of-a-kind gaming experiences for Beginners, Intermediates, Semi-professionals and Professionals with our newest model, the Longitudinal Star Gate 14 Model, Model III. We understand the need to attain balances between pleasure and intellectual stimulation which makes the gaming experiences unforgettable. We deliver the expected and go beyond the unexpected in terms of value with our intricate gaming designs and models which includes but not limited to the intense psychological warfare gaming experiences, Logistics test experiences and intellectual stimulation experiences. These experiences allow players to gain access into the pseudo-dynamic and quasi-kinetic World of Chess. The journey awaits. Embark on a journey of discovery as you tap into the intellectual tapestry stimulation dynamics of chess gaming and test elastic coefficient of your cognitive capacities. Come discover for yourself why Advanced 3-D Chess Inc. truly is the world's leading expert in the art form of complex intellectual stimulation and intense psychological warfare. We offer Lessons and speaking engagements covering areas of Advanced Logistics Chess Dynamics and Kinematics.

The essence of this book intends to synergize the Cognition Informatics thought processes of Chess Players to higher levels of mental awareness of alternatives to the game's possibilities which includes the Triple Set Games. Three-Dimensional Chess offers beneficial effects. Most prominent of these include higher levels of cognitive cognition which improves a Player's mental aptitude and capacity to absorb and to absorb new data over time. This benefit aids to reduce the likelihood of age-related dementia which associates with the memory inability to absorb added information. In addition, another beneficial attribute is it allows Players to develop sustainable focus strategies that results from constant practice of 3-Dimensional Chess games. The effect of constant practice increases the level of synaptic electrical activity in the neuro-synaptic spheres of the brain. As a wise conjecture stipulates, "If you don't use it, you lose it."

It is my sincere aspiration that readers worldwide find this book as informative and as interesting as my discovery of the concepts during the compilation and assemblage of the content materials for this book. I hope that it serves as an inspirational catalyst for Chess Enthusiasts in the near and not so distant future.

Because the rules for registering books with the Library of Congress have been amended or that I am now aware, making the process more difficult to attain a Library of Congress Control Number (L.C.C.N.) since this number must be attained BEFORE publishing a book to be visible in the Library of Congress, all my previously published books will not be visible in the Library of Congress because of this ruling that I of which I am now aware. Therefore, my previously published books do not meet the criteria of attaining a Library of Congress Control Number. Thus, I have decided to provide additional information about my previously published books' International Serial Book Numbers (I.S.B.N.) to facilitate an easier search for these books on the web. Those previously published books are much simpler since they discuss only the Single Set Games and only the Double Set Games played on Model II, an Advance chess board game, the Longitudinal Star Gate 14 Model, or the S.G. 14 Model. This book, however, focuses on the Quadruple Set Game (Q.4.1.1) played on Model III. For most chess beginners, my previously published books may surprisingly be much easier to understand and to comprehend since the games played on Model II are fewer (meaning the Single Set Games and the Double Set Games) and therefore less complicated that this current book. Therefore, to facilitate easier access to those previously published books, I have decided to mention their International Serial Book Numbers, their Titles and their Subtitles as a search guidance outline below:

Book 1 Vol. 1 – The Single Set Games
ISBN-10(ASIN):   1503269485   Website: (https://www.ISBN.1503269485.com)
Title: Advance 3-D Matrix Chess: The Long. S.G. 14 – Single Set Games, Book One, Vol. 1.
Subtitle: The Longitudinal Star Gate 14 Model, Model III: An In-Depth Perspective of Sequential Conglomerates Informatics.
Pages: 190

Book 1 Vol. 2 – The Single Set Games
ISBN-10(ASIN):   1505573378   Website: (https://www.ISBN.1505573378.com)
Title: Renaissance To The Dawn Of A New Age, Single Set Games, Book One, Vol. 2.
Subtitle: A Qualitative Validation for the Art of Psychological Warfare.
Pages: 154

Book 2 Vol. 1 – The Double Set Game   (D.2.10)
ISBN-10(ASIN):   1507648014   Website: (https://www.ISBN.1507648014.com)
Title: Advance Chess: Inferential Analysis of Distributive Cognitive Logistics.
Subtitle: Hybridization of Poly-Plextics Probabilities.
Pages: 190

Book 2 Vol. 2 - The Double Set Game   (D.2.30)
ISBN-10(ASIN):   1514136171   Website: (https://www.ISBN.1514136171.com)
Title: Advance Chess: Inferential View Analysis- The Double Set Game Robotic Intelligence.
Subtitle: Double Set Game – Book 2 Vol. 2.
Pages: 152

Book 2 Vol. 3 - The Double Set Game   (D.2.50)
ISBN-10(ASIN):   1515309207   Website: (https://www.ISBN.1515309207.com)
Title: Advance Chess: Compilations Pertaining To Random Access Problematic Probabilities.
Subtitle: The Synthesis Postulates of the Hybridization Polymerization of Matrix Poly-Plextics Informatics.
Pages: 190

Book 2 Vol. 4 - The Double Set Game (D.4.2.11)
ISBN-10(ASIN):   1518655459   Website: (https://www.ISBN.1518655459.com)
Title: Advance Chess: Extrapolative Insights of the Double Set Game.
Subtitle: Matrix Logistics Poly-Plextics Informatics.
Pages: 174

Book 2 Vol. 5 - The Double Set Game   (D.4.2.31)
ISBN-10(ASIN):   1544787456   Website: (https://www.ISBN.1544787456.com)
Title: Advance Chess- Quiet Reflections of the Double Set Game.
Subtitle: The Symbiosis of Full Spectrum Inferences.
Pages: 112

Book 2 Vol. 6 -   The Double Set Game   (D.4.2.51)
ISBN-10(ASIN):   1977988989   Website: (https://www.ISBN.1977988989.com)
Title: Advance Chess: Relative Retroactive Retrospection of the Double Set Game.
Subtitle: Analysis of (D.4.2.51), Book 2 Vol. 6.
Pages: 194

Book I – The Star Fish Model
ISBN-13:   9791645571865   ISBN-10(ASIN):   B0866C6MN9
Website: (https://www.ISBN.B0866C6MN9.com).
Title: Model I – The Star Fish Model – Single Set/ Single Platform Games (S.S./S.P.1.1 G(1-3), Book 1 Vol. 1 Games (1-3).
Subtitle: A New Horizon for Advance Chess.
Library of Congress Control Number (L.C.C.N.):   2019901586

Book II – The Star Fish Model
ISBN-13:   9781952011443   ISBN-10(ASIN):   B0872G7QTX
Website: (https://www.ISBN.B0872G7QTX.com).
Title: Model I – The Star Fish Model – Single Set / Single Platform Games (S.S./S.P. 1.1.G(4-6), Book 1 Vol. 1 Games (4-6).
Subtitle: Advance Chess Games Anyone ?
Library of Congress Control Number (L.C.C.N.):   2019918138
Pages: 147

Book III – The Star Fish Model
ISBN-13:   9781952894015   ISBN-10(ASIN):   1952894018
Website: (https://www.ISBN.1952894018.com).
Title: Model I – The Star Fish Model – Single Set / Single Platform Games, Book 1 Vol. 1 Games (7-8), (S.S./S.P. 1.1. G (7-8)).
Subtitle: The Symphonic Bases of Advance Chess.
Library of Congress Control Number (LC.C.N.):   2019919000
Pages: 127

Book IV – The Star Fish Model
ISBN-13:   9781952894343   ISBN-10(ASIN):   1952894344
Website: (https://www.ISBN.1952894344.com).
Title: Model I – Single Set/Single Platform Games, Book 1 Vol. 1 Games (9-10), (S.S./S.P.1.1 G(9-10).
Subtitle: Advance Chess for Dummies.
Library of Congress Control Number (LC.C.N.):   2019919457
Pages: 147

Book V – The Star Fish Model
ISBN-13:   9781952894091   ISBN-10(ASIN):   1952894093
Website: (https://www.ISBN.1952894093.com).
Title: Advance Chess – Model I – The Double Set/Single Platform Game, Book 2 Vol. 1 Game # 1, (D.S/S.P. 2.1. G1).
Subtitle: Tactics of Advance Chess. Book 2 Vol. 1 Game# 1
Library of Congress Control Number (LC.C.N.):   2020905683
Pages: 110

Book # 1 – (T.3.1.G1)
         - The Longitudinal Star Gate 14 Model, Model III
ISBN-13:   978-1970160079   ISBN-10(ASIN):   1970160071
Website: (https://www.ISBN.1970160071.com).
Title: Advance Chess – Model III, The Triple Set Game, Book 3 Vol. 1 Game # 1, (T.3.1.G1), (G-G)/(G-G)/(A-A).
Subtitle: Monumental Transformational Subliminal Analysis.
Library of Congress Control Number (L.C.C.N.):   2020911689
Pages: 97

CUSTOM MADE GAME BOARD DESCRIPTION AND PRICING

Special Note: When buying the Advance 3-D Matrix Chess - The Longitudinal Star Gate 14 Model, Model III, Single Set Games, Book 1, Vol. 1 - by Siafa B. Neal, please purchase his custom game board (chess pieces included) so you can enjoy playing the games scripted in this book.

Classic 4 Wings Game Board Set # 1: This custom-made chess board folds up for easy storage and is designed for gamers on the go. The set includes the color coded (Orange-Blue/ Orange-Red / Red-Purple or other assorted colors) chess pieces (choking hazard for children under age 5).

Price $35.00 plus shipping. Please note that all sales are final (no refunds).

Classic 4 Wings Game Board Set #2: This custom-made chess board (made from a light-weight material) is especially designed for all advanced competitive gamers. The set includes the color coded (Orange-Blue/ Orange-Red / Red-Purple or other assorted colors) chess pieces (choking hazard for children under age 5).

Price $200.00 plus shipping. Please note that all sales are final (no refunds).

To order please contact author/inventor Siafa B. Neal by email: chessplayer3334@gmail.com

Please include in your email:
1. Your full name.
2. Which game board set (number) you are requesting.
3. How many game board sets you are requesting?
4. Your full shipping address with zip code.
5. Your contact phone number.

After your email is received you will receive a Pay Pal Invoice (they take e-checks, debit, and all major credit cards). Please allow adequate shipping time and know that we are here to answer all your questions.

Hire 3-D Chess Grand-Master Siafa B. Neal to Advance Your Chess Skills
- Private Lesson: Advance 3-D Chess Grand Master- $ 20 per hour.

Lecture and Game Play Time Slots Available
- 8 Hours or Less Time Slot - $ 160.00
- 12 Hours or Less Time Slot - $ 240.00

In addition to the fees above please include $2,000.00 for travel and accommodation.

Due to high demand all appointments must be scheduled 30 days in advance. All payments are made in advance through Pay Pal.

Please email to schedule with 3-D Chess Grand Master Siafa B. Neal: chessplayer3334@gmail.com

Please include in your email:
1. Your full name
2. The date or dates that you are requesting (please try to schedule 30 days prior to engagement)
3. Full address (location) of Private Lesson, Lecture or Game Event
4. Arrival Time Request
5. Contact phone number
6. No refunds after engagement are scheduled

After your email is received you will receive a Pay Pal Invoice (they take e-checks, debit, and all major credit cards). We are here to answer all your questions.

INTRODUCTION TO INTERNATIONAL CHESS TOURNAMENTS

The first International Chess Tournament did happen in London in 1851. (Footnote 1). Today, both men and women are eligible to contest the title in the World Chess Championship to determine the world champion in the board game chess. Viswanathan Anand, who is currently the world chess champion, won against his challenger Vladimir Krasnik in the World Chess Championship 2008 and again against Vaseline Taplin in the World Chess Championship 2010. (Footnote 2). In addition, there is a separate competitions and titles for juniors, seniors, and computers. Currently there is a restriction on the use of computers to compete for the open title.

On November 7 – 25, 2014, in the Russian city of Sochi, the World Chess Championship took place between World Champion Magnus Carlsen and Challenger Vishy Anand. Magnus Carlsen (Norway), defending his title for the first time, an incumbent World Chess Champion since 2013, is the youngest player ever to become a Grand-Master. Recognized as "The Mozart of chess" by fans and media alike, he is known for his amazing chess skills in the end game. Viswanathan Anand (India) who was a five times World Chess Champion, is one of the most versatile chess players in the world. He is the only world champion who won chess titles playing in all different formats such as matches, tournaments, and knockouts. Vishy is the first Indian Grandmaster (http://www.sochi2014.fide.com).

Today over six hundred million people play chess. The Championship match, which is watched by over 3 million people from all over the world, is a culmination of a two-year FIDE cycle played every two years between the incumbent Champion and the winner of the Candidates tournament. The winner of the match which is played over a maximum of twelve games is the first player to score 6.5 points or more. If the scores are even after twelve games, a four tie-break is played. (Footnote 3).

Chess tournaments today are the standard form of chess competition amongst avid players. Some of the most recognized chess tournaments regarding individual competition include the Linares chess tournament and the Tata Steel chess tournament, to name a few. The Chess Olympiad is the largest team chess tournament; in this regard, players compete for their country's team in an equivalent manner as the Olympic Games (Footnote 4).

The World Chess Federation, Federation Internationale des Echecs (FIDE) organizes and rules most chess tournaments in accordance with its published handbook. This handbook offers guidelines and regulations for conducting tournaments. To determine the winning participant(s), chess tournaments may use the round-robin style, the Swiss system, or the elimination style of play (Footnote 5).

Since the establishment of modern chess around 1475, the first structure competition (tournament) did not occur until 1841 in Leeds (Footnote 6). In 1849, there was a finalist tournament in London and likewise in 1851 a winner's tournament in Amsterdam (Footnotes 7,8). It was during the Great Exhibition, which served as a guide for future international chess tournaments that the 1851 London tournament did occur. The London tournament did suffer from drawbacks because of the lack of a finalist elimination tournament format and the need for time controls (chess clocks) (Footnote 9). The winner of the 1851 London tournament was Adolf Andersen, the chess player from Germany whom the world regarded as the best chess player during that time (Footnote 10,11).

There was an exponential rapid exploding growth of international chess tournaments after the 1851 London tournament. Towards the end of the 1850's ubiquitous chess tournaments expanded world-wide to cities such as Berlin, Paris, Manchester, New York, San Francisco, Birmingham, and Vienna (Footnotes 12,13,14).

CHESS OLYMPIAD

In 1924, there was a request to include chess at the Olympic Games. There was a denial of this request since it was problematic to distinguish an amateur chess player from a professional chess player. This problem was one of the leading problems for the cancellation of this proposal event (Footnote 15). The establishment of the first unofficial Chess

Olympiad in Paris occurred separately from the 1924 Summer Paris Olympics also during that year (Footnote 16). The formation of the Federation Internationale des Echecs (FIDE) took place towards the closing day of the unofficial chess Olympiad (Footnote 17). In 1927, FIDE organized the first official Chess Olympiad that involved sixteen participating countries (Footnote 15). This number continues to grow so that in 1990 during the twenty-nineth Chess Olympiad 127-member countries were participating in the event (Footnote 18). Until 1950, FIDE continued to sponsor the Chess Olympiads at irregular intervals; thereafter, events of the tournament continue regularly every two years (Footnote 19).

CURRENT INTRODUCTION TO COMPUTER CHESS MATCH

According to Jennifer Larsen's Time magazine's article, "Did Deep Blue Beat Kasparov Because of a System Glitch?", (retrieval date 07/25/15 at 2:15 P.M.), which posts on February 17, 2015, claims that chess champion, Gary Kasparov, could defeat the IBM supercomputer "Deep Blue" in a six-game chess match (Footnote 20). Gary Kasparov comments in an essay to Time magazine's article, "The Day that I sensed a new Kind of Intelligence, "(Monday, March 25,1996), that he prefers all or nothing when he scoffs at an offer to split the $500,000 purse 60-40 between winner and loser of a computer chess challenge match (Footnote 21). Gary receives his "first glimpse of Artificial Intelligence on February 10,1996 at 4:45 P.M. E.S.T. "when in the first game match with Deep Blue, the computer sacrifices a White pawn to tactically fracture Black pawn structure and to create an opening on the board (Footnote 22, para. (1)). Gary further comments that, "although there did not appear to be a forced line of play, that would allow recovery of the pawn, my instincts told me that with so many "loose" Black pawns and a somewhat exposed Black King, White could probably recover the material, with a better overall position to boot," (Footnote 22). Furthermore, Gary remarks, "But a computer, I thought, would never make such a move," and comments that, "A Computer can't "see" the long-term consequences of structural changes in the position or understand how the changes in pawn formations may be good or bad", (Footnote 22, para. (2)).

Gary further states that, "Humans do this sort of thing all the time. But computers generally calculate each line of play so far as possible within the time allocated". Commenting further, Gary remarks that, "Because chess is a game of virtually limitless possibilities, even a beast like Deep Blue, which can look at more than 100 million positions a second, can go only so deep. When computers reach that point, they evaluate the various resulting positions and select the move leading to the best one". Adding further, "and because computers' primary way of evaluating chess positions is by measuring material superiority, they are notoriously materialistic. If they "understood" the game, they might act differently, but they don't understand," (Footnote 22). Suggesting, "So I was stunned by this pawn (White) sacrifice." Asking to himself, "What could it mean?" Again remarking, "I had played a lot of computers but had never experienced anything like this. I could feel- I could smell – a new kind of intelligence across the table. While I played through the rest of the game as best as I could, I was lost; it played beautiful, flawless chess the rest of the way and won easily," (Footnote 22, para. (4) , retrieved 07/25/15 at 11:15 P.M.).

Surmising, "Later I discovered the truth. Deep Blue's computational powers were so great that it did in fact calculate every possible move all the way to the actual recovery of the pawn six move later. The computer didn't view the pawn sacrifice as a sacrifice at all. So, the question is, "If the computer makes the same move that I would make for completely different reasons, has it made an "intelligent" move? Is the intelligence of an action dependent on who (or what) takes it?" (Footnote 22, para. (5)).

Adding, "This is a philosophical question I did not have time to answer. When I understood what had happened, however, I was reassured. In fact, I was able to exploit the traditional shortcomings of computers throughout the rest of the match. At one point, for example, I changed slightly the order of a well-known opening sequence." Suggesting further, "Because it was unable to compare this new position meaningfully with similar ones in its database, it had to start calculating away and was unable to find a good plan. A human would have wondered, "What's Gary up to?", judged the change to be meaningless and moved on," (Footnote 22, para.(6)).

Concluding, " Indeed my overall thrust in the last five games was to avoid giving the computer any concrete goal to calculate toward; if it can't find a way to win material, attack the kind or fulfill one of its other programmed priorities, the computer drifts and gets into trouble. In the end, which may have been my biggest advantage: I could figure out its priorities and adjust my play. It couldn't do the same to me. So, although I think I did see some signs of intelligence, it's a weird kind, an inefficient, inflexible kind that makes me think I have (still) a few years left", (Footnote 22, para. (7)). After his initial loss, in the first-time match with Deep Blue, winning three matches and drawing two, Kasparov wasn't ready to give up on the human race – or himself (Footnote 23).

According to Time magazine, the next year Gary plays a new and superior version of Deep Blue but did not win the match, although easily winning the first game. Deep Blue superior program enables its domination of the second game (Footnote 24). The loss visibly disturbs Kasparov who sighs, rubbing his face, before he abruptly stands and walks away, thereby forfeiting the match (Footnote 25). Gary later states that, "he was again riled by the computer move that uses so surprising, so un-machine-like, that he was sure the IBM team had cheated." According to Time magazine, the actual cause may have been a glitch in Deep Blue's programming: Faced with too many options and no clear preference, the computer makes a random move. The move that causes Kasparov to lose, was not a feature, but in fact, a bug (Footnote 26).

HISTORY: COMPUTERS IN CHESS T OURNAMENTS

According to Wikipedia, (https://en.wikipedia.org/wiki/chess_tournament), the first chess engine, that is to say, a chess playing computer program, to defeat a person a person in a tournament occurs in 1967 by the program, Mac Hack Six (Footnote 27). After this event there were tournaments specifically for chess computers. In 1970, New York City sponsors the first North American Computer Chess Championship (NACCC). Later Stockholm, in 1974, sponsors the first World Computer Chess Championship (WCC). The world recognizes KAISSA, the Soviet Union's chess program as the world's first computer chess champion (Footnote 28/29). In 1995, Paderborn, Germany sponsors the world's first Computer Speed Chess Championship for blitz chess. Later, top commercial programs, which include Shredder or Fritz surpass world champion players in challenging games with brief time controls. Since 2007, Rybak, continue to dominate every World Computer Chess Championship. The revocation of its titles later occurs upon the discovery of the program's plagiarism of other types of computer chess program. Since then, other champion level computer programs that later dominates the game includes Fritz, HIARCS, Junior, Shredder, and Zappa (Footnote 30).

PRESENT

In 1996, Gary Kasparov, the world chess champion, challenges the IBM super chess computer, IBM RS/6000 SP or "Deep Blue". Time magazine reports that Kasparov calls this machine, "the monster", at which time, during the challenge tournament, Kasparov, spends much of the week grimacing and holds his head in frustration sitting across the chess board from an IBM scientist taking instructions from Deep Blue. As the match turns out, Kasparov wins the match, while Deep Blue only wins one of the games. The computer's only victory marks the first time that a computer is victorious under chess tournament Rules and conditions (Footnote 31). An upgrade to Deep Blue having evolution capabilities of two hundred million chess positions per second wins a rematch against Kasparov in 1997 (Footnote 32).

Before the Deep Blue upgrade match, Kasparov comments, "In the article I wrote for Time (magazine) last year after my victorious match against IBM's Deep Blue supercomputer in Philadelphia, I expressed my surprise and amazement at seeing a kind of intelligence. I referred to Game 1, in which the computer's decision to sacrifice a pawn, based strictly on the machine's calculations, coincided with what a human would have done using human logic" (Footnote 32, ibid). After losing to the Deep Blue upgrade program match, Kasparov, comments, "Unfortunately, I based my preparation for this match, played two weeks ago in New York City, on the conventional wisdom of what would constitute good anti-computer strategy." Adding, "Conventional wisdom is - or was until the end of the match

– to avoid early confrontations, play a slow game, try to out-maneuver the machine, force positional mistakes, and then, when the climax comes, not lose your concentration and not make an any tactical mistakes." Lamenting his loss in the match, he comments, "It was my bad luck that this strategy worked perfectly in Game 1 – but never again for the rest of the match. By the middle of the match, I found myself unprepared for what turned out to be a totally new kind of intellectual challenge". Adding further, "The decisive game of the match was Game 2, which left a scar in my memory and prevented me from achieving my usual total concentration in the following games. In Deep Blue's Game 2, we saw something that went well beyond our wildest expectations of how well a computer would be able to foresee the long-term positional consequence of its decisions. The machine refused to move to a position that had a decisive short-term advantage - showing a very human sense of danger. I think this moment could mark a revolution in computer science that could earn IBM and the Deep Blue team a Noble Prize. Even today, weeks later, no other chess playing program in the world has been able to evaluate correctly the consequences of Deep Blue's position". Further suggesting, "Also, Game 2 had a very unfortunate finish. Deep Blue held a strategically winning position, but it made a tactical blunder that, if I had sacrificed a piece, could have given me a miraculous escape. But I trusted the machine's calculations, thinking it would not miss such a continuation, and resigned instead."

Later suggesting, "Game 2 created an enigma for me that I never solved and from which I never recovered. I would like the IBM team to start disclosing the secrets of how they achieved this unthinkable success in chess programing. They claim they developed software that enables them to change the style of the program mid-match and the evaluation ability of the machine from game to game. This also is revolutionary, because any changes, any tweak in the computer normally need weeks of testing to avoid potential bugs. Adding, "I discovered that I was playing a very flexible, quickly changing opponent with an ability to avoid any mistakes in long-term calculations. My opponent was psychologically stable, undisturbed, and unconcerned about anything going on around it, and it made almost none of the typical computer-chess errors. Further adding, "Now I would like to look to the future. I think we have to separate science and sport. I believe the IBM team owes the world of chess, and the world of science, a full explanation of how such a flexible machine was developed. They have to make all the scientific data available to allow others to judge their accomplishment". Still commenting, "I also think IBM owes me, and all of mankind, a rematch. I hereby challenge IBM to a match of ten games, 20 days long, to play every second day. I would like to have access in advance to the log of 10 Deep Blue games played with a neutral player of another computer in the presence of my representative. I would like to play this fall, when I can be in my best form after a summer of vacation and preparation. And I'm ready to play for all or nothing, winner take all, just to show that it's not about money. Moreover, I think it would be advisable if IBM would step down as an organizer of the match. It should be organized independently." Suggesting further, "I think IBM was the big winner of this match. It scored many points in advertising and in the stock market. I also think the company owes something to chess. I think it would be great if IBM contributed to chess development; specifically, it could create scholarship to help talented kids study chess." Also adding, "I think this match proved that there should be no special anti-computer strategy. To beat this machine, I just have to play great chess. I need comprehensive, bullet-proof opening preparation that checks all sharp lines of play to avoid any flaws – which can be deadly when playing Deep Blue. I need physical and psychological stability, a great level of concentration and a mind free of other distractions to calculate, calculate and calculate." Concluding, "I think something great is happening. I'm proud to be part of that. But I don't want to be a loser because I'm playing only at 50% of my capacity and 50% of my psychological stability. If we get this rematch, I'm ready, whatever the outcome, to go to IBM's labs and have a nice talk with the Deep Blue team. But until then, I'm going to treat them as a very hostile opponent, in order to be ready for the toughest challenge of my life" (Footnote 33).

SHOULD CHESS BE AN OLYMPIC SPORT?

Meaghan Haier's Time magazine article, " Should Chess Be an Olympic Sport?", (retrieved date 09/27/15 at 3:35 P.M.),which posts on Tuesday, August 05,2008, (http://content.time.com/time/world/article/0,8599,1827716,00.

html) discusses the issue of chess becoming an Olympic Sport and asks the question, " What makes an Olympic Sport?". In the article, Meaghan claims that the games which gets the official nod from the International Olympic Committee (I.O.C.) may be controversial and sometimes bewildering as to how the Committee selects the types of sports to be registered for the Olympic games. The article suggests for example that the Olympic Committee considers rhythmic gymnastics as an Olympic sport, however, ballroom dancing is not. The article continues to exclaim that handball and badminton are a part of the program and suggests that rugby and squash are not included in the Olympic game programs. The article further claims that amongst the 28 sports that meets the approval of the Committee for the year 2012 table tennis is inclusive in the program whereas, golf, baseball, softball or racquetball are not included in the Olympic sporting events.

According to Kiran Ilyumzhinov, president of the World Chess Federation (FIDE),who claims that, curbing which is simply, "chess on ice, and it is an Olympic sport, but classical chess is not!", has been attempting for decades to get the board game of chess, a "sport of the mind", approval by the I.O.C. but with little success. Likewise, the World Bridge Federation (WBF), which represents the card game of bridge, and which attempts to receive I.O.C. approval since 1995 receive denial responses from the I.O.C. Both organizations, FIDE and WBF in their efforts to gain approval from the I.O.C. offers to submit their players to drug testing in affirmation to the Olympics' anti-doping code standards but only to receive negative responses and denials from the I.O.C. (Footnote 34). Both FIDE and WBF views are that gaining recognition as an official Olympic sport would be beneficial to the Olympic games, raising their profiles, status and awareness of the chess and bridge card game to higher levels of consciousness and involvement in countries where they do not get government funding. Despite continuous rejection, FIDE attempts to sue the I.O.C. in the Court of Arbitration for Sports which oversees international sports disputes in Lausanne, Switzerland but later rescinds. Peter Rajanya, the public-relations director of FIDE, claims that "our strength is not in the court" and that FIDE is now in "the process of serious negotiations [with the IOC] and improving relations". Rajanya further states that to attain this objective, the chess organization launches an open office in Lausanne with the goal of getting closer to IOC officials, as well as promoting chess as an international sport (Footnote 36).

IOC views adding official sports to the Games to be a complex matter, in part, because of the overgrown size of the event. According to Emmanuelle Moreau, the IOC spokesperson, the Olympic Games are already so large that cities may not be able to accommodate them in terms of building infrastructure (hotel accommodations), transportation infrastructure (roads, buses, rail, airports) and entertainment industry (museums, art galleries, theatres, sporting stadiums). As a result of this problem of being over-sized and or over-sizing, when IOC president Jacques Rogge assume office in 2001, he limits the number of sporting events to 35, whereby 28 sporting events occur in summer and 7 occur in winter as well as implements a regular review process to avoid further expanding the Olympic program. Through Jacques-Rogge management the IOC presently votes on new sports and reviews existing ones, on the bases of through technical analysis and specific criteria, after each Olympic event; the Beijing Games was last to include baseball and softball however, the IOC deletes them in the year of 2012. In 1995 and 1999 IOC grants the bridge game and the chess organizations as "Recognized International Sports Federations" status respectively but says it does not accept either game into the official registry because they both (the bridge card game and the chess game) lack the essential feature of physical activity. According to Moreau, IOC spokeswoman, "mind sports, by their nature, cannot be part of the program", and further suggests that the IOC does not reject their bid entirely (Footnote 36).

Rajanya claims that "In the ancient Olympic Games, the element of cultural and mental activity was present". Contests in music, theater, poetry, and other arts were inclusive during the ancient Olympic Games. He adds, "In the Olympic Games, until the Second World War, there were competitions that rewarded physical efforts. Today, the missing element of the intellectual competition can be reintroduced by the involvement of chess, and bridge" (Footnote 37). Dan Morse, secretary of WBF and president of the American Contract Bridge League thinks that bridge enthusiasts would disagree with the characterization of the card game as a nonphysical activity. He claims that "We think bridge is a sport. It requires stamina, brain power and concentration…Bridge is a sport just like baseball and football. It requires training and strenuous exercise. It is more than just a game." According to the Time article, "Should Chess be an Olympic Sport?", the national Olympic committees of some countries already accept bridge as an official sport. Before the 2012 Salt Lake City Olympics, WBF establishes an exhibition competition whereas the chess federation maintains two similar matches in the 2000 Sydney Games (Footnote 38).

In the fall of 2008, bridge and chess players compete in the first-ever World Mind Sports Games in Beijing. The competition which maintains over 3,000 competitors from at least 150 nations competes for thirty-five gold medals in chess, bridge, draughts (checkers), Go and Xiang qi (a Chinese version of chess) at the site. According to Rajanya, the Mind Games will "show to the World that these games require effort, competence and determination just like any other sport" and "can bring joy, happiness and spectacle to the participants and to the audience." Georgios Markopoulos, the deputy president of FIDE and the International Mind Sports Association agrees, further commenting: "We hope that this event in Beijing will be so important and so big that the IOC will understand that they need us,"(Footnote 39).

CHESS NEWS:

" Chess Champion Touts Benefits of AI, Downplays Fears".

According to Helen Christophe's article, "Chess Champion Touts Benefits of AI, Downplays Fears", The Courthouse News, published on May 10, 2018 (retrieved on 05/11/18 at 9:35 P.M.), Gary Kasparov, who was defeated by a chess-playing computer in 1977, commented that it is time for people to reject the "mythological" feat that artificially intelligent killer robots would annihilate humanity and that people should collaborate with AI to advance scientific discovery. In his keynote address at the Train AI conference in San Francisco, Kasparov comments, "How about bringing together the best of two worlds: human creativity, our fantasy, our ability to strategize and machine brute-force calculating." Further commenting, "It is time for us to start reconsidering these relations and find the best way of incorporating with machines."

The Helen's article mentions that artificial intelligence (computer systems capable of intelligent behavior) is becoming ubiquitous. The papers further claim that artificial intelligence is found in a range of applications ranging from search engines and spam filters to automatic speech recognition and medical image analysis tools. Also, the technology is also included and embedded in self-driving cars and drones for disaster relief operations. Looking ahead, the technology could speed scientific research and help develop cures for deadly diseases.

Despite all the positive attributes that artificial intelligence brings other experts in that area fear that if artificial intelligence surpasses human intelligence, it could drive us to extinction. In 2014, Stephen Hawking, a famous Cosmologist, warned that the advent of super intelligent machines would be "the biggest event in human history". Further adding, that "It might also be the last unless we learn to avoid the risks." The article goes on to say that for example if a super-intelligent system is given the task of curing cancer, it might conclude that the only way to do so would be to kill every person on earth. Also, that if was free of human control due to its superior intelligence, the system would set about its gruesome task.

According to Helen Christophe's article, most experts agree that machine intelligence would surpass human intelligence within a century. On the other hand, Kasparov dismisses those fears saying that it was "science fiction." Kasparov who writes and lectures on the intersection of human and machine intelligence, instead envisions a future in which human and machines collaborate to make advances that would otherwise be impossible. It is Kasparov understanding that a human "operator" would set the framework within which a machine must solve a problem. According to Kasparov, humanity preeminence would be preserved if for instance, the operator does not properly define the framework then the machine's results would be useless. Also, Kasparov thinks that jobs and industries will evolve and adapt as robots become smarter. Thus, human operators will require less training and expertise to oversee them (Footnote 40).

SECTION A

Model III: The Longitudinal (Horizontal) Star Gate 14 Model

The development of the Longitudinal Star Gate 14 model or Long.S.G.14 model facilitates the need to include pizzazz and intricacy in the rather boring, mundane game of conventional classical chess. The Longitudinal Star Gate 14 model is an exponential hybrid variant derivative of the Star Fish (Photo 1 shows the Star Fish model). The difference between the two mentioned models is that the Star Gate 14 model is an asymmetric duplex replication of the Star Fish model. Primarily the initial set-up position configuration of the chess pieces on both models may take two forms. These forms are: (1) Linear positioning and (2) Non-Linear positioning.

Photo 1 shows the Top View of an initial Uniform, Linear positioning set-up configuration of the chess pieces. Player I control the Red color band White pieces at the bottom of the game board. Player II controls the Red color band Black pieces at the top or opposite end of the game board. This set-up is Uniform because the chess set positions on a single-layer game Platform. Photo 2 shows a close-up Right View of a Uniform, Linear positioning set-up configuration for a Single Set game on a single-layer game Platform.

Photo 3 shows the Top View of an initial Uniform, Non-Linear positioning set-up configuration for a Single Set game on a single-layer Platform. Photo 4 shows the Right View close-up of an initial Uniform, Non-Linear positioning set-up for a Single Set game on a single-layer Platform.

The S.G. 14 model differs from the Star Fish model because the S.G. 14 model may occur in two structural forms. These forms are: (1) the Latitudinal (two vertically perpendicular Star Fish models) and (2) the Longitudinal (two horizontal asymmetric Star Fish models).

A conventional chess board consists of Rows and Columns. Diagram 1 shows a Conventional Chess board. The enumeration of the Rows is from numbers 1-8 starting at the Bottom Row #1 and ascending to the Top Row #8. The Column label starts with the letter "A" at the extreme Left of the board and ends with the letter "H" at the extreme Right of the board.

Diagram 2 shows the position of the chess pieces on a Conventional Chess board. Player I white pieces position on all the squares that constitute both Row 1 and Row 2. Player II black pieces station on all the squares that constitute Row 7 and Row 8. Notice that Player I white Queen positions on the white square at "Q 1D", the number "1" represents the Row at which Player I white Queen locates, and the letter "D" indicates the Column at which the Queen situates. Player II black Queen stations at the opposite side of the game board at "Q 8D"; also, the number "8" represents the Row on the Board at which the Player II black Queen stations and the letter "D" indicates the Column of its location on a conventional chess game board. It is wise to note that a Queen always positions on the square of its color during the initial set-up at the start of a game. For example, a white Queen must position on the white square at the start of a game and likewise a black Queen should station on the black square also at the start of a game.

Diagram.3 depicts the initial Movements of the chess pieces of a Single Set game on a conventional game board. The Yellow color shade indicates Player I chess piece movements. The Blue color shade depicts Player II chess piece movements. The letter "Kn" represents the Knights; the movement of the Knight displaces in a 3/2 squares Forward Advance movement. The letter "B" stands for the Bishops; this piece moves diagonally across the game board. The letter "Q" indicates the Queens and the letter "Ki" represents the Kings. The objective of the game is to capture or remove an opponent's King.

The Equations below represent the initial movements of a sample Single Set game on a single-layer conventional chess board of Diagram 3.

1. I w (P2A-P4A); II b (P7B - P5B)
2. I w (Kn1B-Kn3C); II b (B8C-B6A)
3. I w (P2D-P4D); II b (PB7-P6C)

4. I w (P2G-P4G); II b (P7E-P6E)
5. I w (Kn1G-Kn3H)

Equation 1 states:
1. I w (P2A-P4A); II b (P7B-P5B)
This means that:
In Equation 1, part 1, Player I White Pawn that positions at Row (2), Column (A) or (P 2A) advances forward two spaces to Row (4), Column (A) or (P4A).
In Equation 1, part 2, Player II responds by moving the Black Pawn that stations at Row (7), Column (B) or (P7B) to Row (5), Column (B) or (P5B).

Equation 2 states:
2. I w (Kn1B-Kn3C); II b (B8C-B6A)
This means that:
In Equation 2, part 1, Player I White Knight that positions at Row (1), Column (B) or (Kn 1B) uses the 3/2 squares Forward Advance movement to advance to Row (3), Column (C) or (Kn3C).
In Equation 2, part 2, Player II responds by moving the Black Bishop that stations at Row (8), Column (C) or (B8C) diagonally to Row (6), Column (A) or (B6A).

Equation 3 states:
3. I w (P2D-P4D); II b (PB7-P6C)
This means that:
In Equation 3, part 1, Player I White Pawn that positions at Row (2), Column (D) or (P 2D) uses the two spaces Forward Advance movement to displace to Row (4), Column (D) or (P4D).
In Equation 3, part 2, Player II Black Pawn that stations at Row (B), Column (7) or (PB7) uses the single space Forward Advance movement to displace to Row (6), Column (C) or (P6C).

Equation 4 states:
4. I w (P2G-P4G); II b (P7E-P6E)
This means that:
In Equation 4, part 1, Player I White Pawn that positions at Row (2), Column (G) or (P2G) uses the two spaces Forward Advance movement to displace to Row (4), Column (G) or (P4G).
In Equation 4, part 2, Player II Black Pawn that stations at Row (7), Column (E) or (P7E) uses the single space Forward Advance movement to displace to Row (6), Column (E) or (P6E).
Equation 5 states:
5. I w (Kn1G-Kn3H)
This means that:
In Equation 5, part 1, Player I White Knight that positions at Row (1), Column (G) or (Kn 1G) uses the 3/2 squares Forward Advance movement to displace to Row (3), Column (H) or (Kn3H).

The Latitudinal Star Gate 14 model derives its structure from the Cubic chess model; the cubic chess model has double layers that are perpendicular to each other. Diagram 4 depicts a Cubic game board of a Single Set chess game having double-layer Platforms. The Bottom layer on the Cubic model is the GROUND Platform that locates a Base (0). The Top layer is the AIR Platform that is situated at Base (1). The initial position set-up configuration for this Single Set game is "GROUND-TO-GROUND "which shows symbolically as (G-G). The chess piece movements for both Players I and II may occur at both layers sporadically, spontaneously, simultaneously, and intermittently.

Diagram 5 presents the initial chess movements of a Single Set game on the Cubic game boards. The game has a (G-G) initial set-up configuration. The color shades indicate the chess piece movements. Diagram 6 presents a Cubic game with a Single Set display having a "GROUND-TO-AIR" (G-A) initial set-up position configuration. Player I pieces position at the Bottom (GROUND) level and Player II pieces station at the Top (AIR) level. This game is a Non-Uniform, Linear Single Set game; the game is non-Uniform since the pieces of the set starts at two different levels.

Diagram 7 displays the Latitudinal Star Gate 14 model. The Bottom layer is the GROUND Platform, and the Top layer is the AIR Platform. This diagram displaying the Latitudinal (Vertical) model shows how the Top layer or Air Zone that situates at Base (1) distinguishes from the Bottom layer or Ground Zone that locates at Base (0). Diagram 7 depicts the layers of the Latitudinal S.G.14 model. The Bottom (GROUND) layer designates as Base (0) and the Top (AIR) layer designates as Base (1). The Center grid or board of the Bottom layer is the Bottom Center which symbolically shows as (B.C.) that locates at Base (0). The Center grid or board of the Top layer is the Top Center which symbolically indicates as (T.C.) that situates at Base (1). Diagram 8 names the various Sections of the Bottom Platform and the Top Platform of the Latitudinal S.G.14 model. Diagram 9 illustrates the Coordinates of the Latitudinal S.G.14 model.

Photo 6 shows the image of the Longitudinal Star Gate 14 model, Model III. This model consists of two Platforms. These are the Top (AIR) Platform, the platform that is closer to you and the Bottom (GROUND) Platform, the platform further away from you. The photo also shows the asymmetric linear relationship of the Top (AIR) layer from the Bottom (GROUND) layer.

Diagram 10 illustrates the Sections and the Coordinates of the Top (AIR) Platform of the Longitudinal Star Gate 14 model. Diagram 11 depicts the Sections and the Coordinates of the Bottom (GROUND) Platform of the Longitudinal Star Gate 14 model. Diagram 12 names the two types of Platforms of the Long.S.G.14 model. Diagram 13 presents the abbreviations for the Sections of the model. Diagram 14 examines the Sections of the model. Diagram 15 displays the Coordinates of the model. Diagram 16 shows the "GROUND-TO-GROUND "initial position set-up configuration for a Single Set, Uniform, linear chess game on the Long.S.G.14 model. Diagram 17 shows the "GROUND-TO-GROUND" initial position set-up configuration for a Single Set, Non-Uniform, linear chess game on the Long.S.G.14 model. See photos on the next few pages.

Photo 1 - Top view of the Star Fish model showing the Single Set, Uniform, Linear positioning setup.

Photo 2 - Close-up Right view of a Single Set, Uniform, Linear position configuration setup.

Photo 3 - Top View of the Star Fish model showing the Single Set, Uniform, Non-Linear positioning configuration setup.

Photo 4 - Close-up Right View of the Star Fish model showing the Single Set, Uniform, Non-Linear positioning setup.

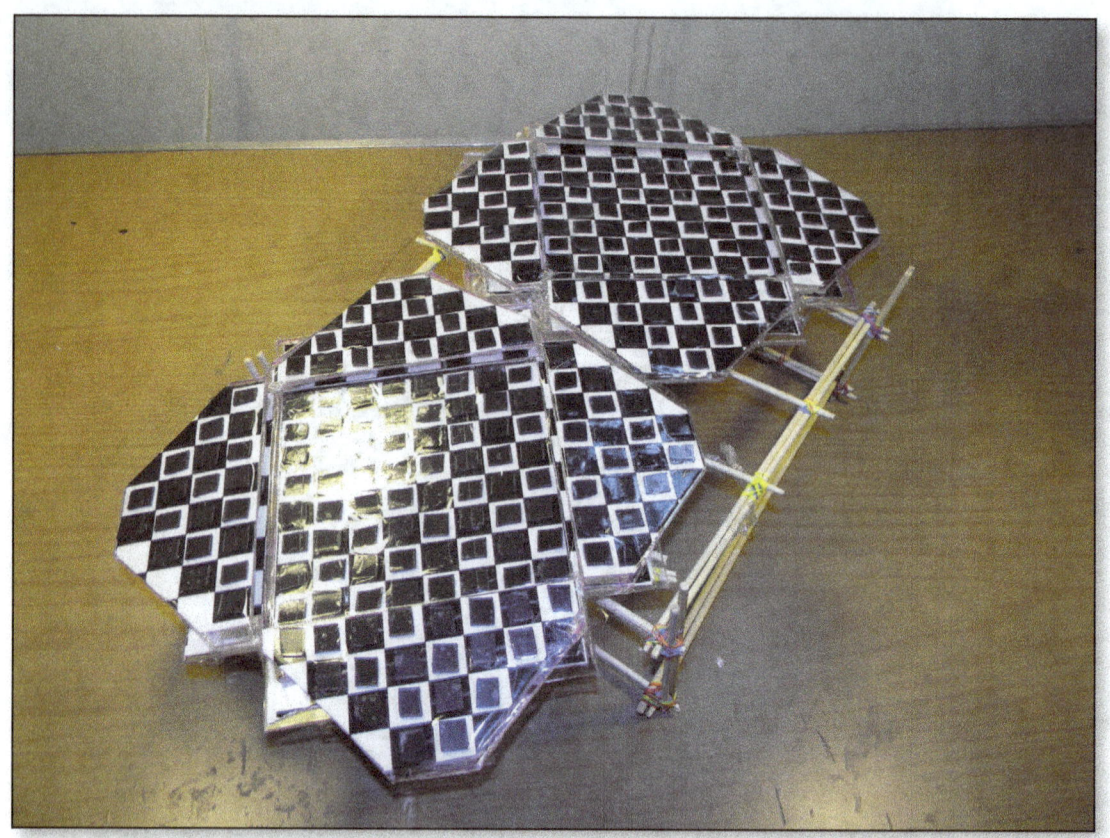

Photo 6 - The Longitudinal Star Gate 14 Model (original).

The list below shows the Possible Position Scenarios of a Single Set Chess game:

<u>**Single Set Mode:**</u>

(G-G) = GROUND-TO-GROUND initial Uniform, Non-Linear position configuration set-up at the Bottom Layer. For example, Player I Orange-Blue color band *white* pieces may be located at the Lower Bottom (L.B.) section at Base (0) of the Bottom Platform. Player II Orange-Blue color band *black* pieces may station at the Upper Bottom (U.B.) section at Base (1) of the Bottom Platform.

(A-A) = AIR-TO-AIR initial Uniform, Non-Linear position configuration set-up at the Top Layer. For example, Player I Orange-Blue color band *white* pieces may position at the Lower Top (L.T.) section at Base (1) of the Top Platform. Player II Orange-Blue color band *black* pieces may station at the Upper Top (U.T.) section also at Base (1) of the Top Platform

(G-A) = GROUND-TO-AIR initial Non-Uniform, Non-Linear position configuration set-up partially at both the Bottom Layer and the Top Layer. For example, Player I Orange-Blue color band *white* pieces may position at the Lower Bottom (L.B.) section at Base (0) of the Bottom Platform. Player II Orange-Blue color band *black* pieces may station at the Upper Top (U.T.) section at Base (1) of the Top Platform.

(A-G) = AIR-TO-GROUND initial Non-Uniform, Non-Linear position configuration set-up partially at both the Bottom Layer and the Top Layer. For example, Player I Orange Blue color band *white* pieces may position at the Lower Top (L.T.) section at Base (1) of the Top Platform. Player II Orange-Blue color band *black* pieces may station at the Upper Bottom (U.B.) section at Base (0) of the Bottom Platform.

Photo 7 presents the GROUND-TO-GROUND (G-G) initial position set-up for a Single Set, Uniform, Non-Linear chess game. Photo 8 shows the GROUND-TO-AIR (G-A) initial position set-up for a Single Set, Non-Uniform, Non-Linear chess game on the Long.S.G.14 model. Photo 9 illustrates the AIR-TO-AIR (A-A) initial position set-up for a Single Set, Uniform, Non-Linear chess game. Photo 10 depicts the AIR-TO-GROUND (A-G) initial position set-up for a Single Set, Non-Uniform, Non-Linear chess game on the Long.S.G.14 model.

Double Set Mode:

Photo 11 presents the GROUND-TO-GROUND/ GROUND-TO-GROUND (G-G) / (G-G) initial setup for the Double Set, Uniform, Non-Linear chess game on the revised version of the Longitudinal Star Gate 14 model; Chess Set # 1 (the Orange-Blue color band set) locates at the (G-G) VERTICAL position and Chess Set # 2 (the Orange-Red color band set) situates also at the (G-G) HORIZONTAL position.

Photo 13 illustrates the AIR-TO-GROUND/GROUND-TO-GROUND (A-G)/(G-G) initial position setup for the Double Set, Non-Uniform, Non-Linear chess game; Chess Set # 1 locates at the (A-G) VERTICAL position and Chess Set # 2 situates at the (G-G) HORIZONTAL position.

Photo 14 depicts the AIR-TO-AIR/GROUND-TO-GROUND (A-A)/(G-G) initial setup for the Double Set, Uniform, Non-Linear chess game; Chess Set # 1 locates at the (A-A) VERTICAL position and Chess Set # 2 situates at the (G-G) HORIZONTAL position.

Photo 15 represents the AIR-TO-AIR/AIR-TO-GROUND (A-A)/(A-G) initial setup for the Double Set, Non-Uniform, Non-Linear chess game; Chess Set # 1 (the Orange-Blue color band set) locates at the (A-A) VERTICAL position and Chess Set # 2 (the Orange-Red color band set) situates at the (A-G) HORIZONTAL position.

Photo 16 reveals the AIR-TO-AIR/AIR-TO-AIR (A-A)/(A-A) initial setup for the Double Set, Uniform, Non-Linear chess game; Chess Set # 1 locates at the (A-A) VERTICAL position and Chess Set # 2 situates at the (A-A) HORIZONTAL position.

Photo 17 discloses the GROUND-TO-AIR/AIR-TO-AIR (G-A)/(A-A) initial setup for the Double Set, Non-Uniform, Non-Linear chess game; Chess Set # 1 locates at the (G-A) VERTICAL position and Chess Set # 2 situates at the (A-A) HORIZONTAL position.

Photo 18 unveils the GROUND-TO-AIR/AIR-TO-GROUND (G-A)/(A-G) initial setup for the Double Set, Non-Uniform, Non-Linear chess game; Chess Set # 1 (the Orange-Blue color band set) locates at the (G-A) VERTICAL position and Chess Set # 2 (the Orange-Red color band set) situates at the (A-G) HORIZONTAL position.

Photo 19 displays the GROUND-TO-AIR/GROUND-TO-GROUND (G-A)/(G-G) initial setup for the Double Set, Non-Uniform, Non-Linear chess game; Chess Set # 1 locates at the (G-A) VERTICAL position and Chess Set # 2 situates at the (G-G) HORIZONTAL position.

Triple Set Mode:

Photo 20 reveals the GROUND-TO-GROUND/GROUND-TO-GROUND/AIR-TO-AIR (G-G)/(G-G)/(A-A) initial setup for the Triple Set (Chess Set #1 = the Orange-Blue color band set, Chess Set # 2 = the Orange-Red color band Set and Chess Set # 3 = the Red-Purple color band set) is a Uniform (because Chess Set # 1 is on the SAME Platform at the GROUND level and Chess Set # 2 is on the SAME Platform at the GROUND level),Non-Linear (the chess pieces have non-linear arrangements) chess game. The nomenclature of the first group of letters (G-G) represents Chess Set # 1, the second group of letters (G-G-) represents Chess Set # 2 and the third group of letters (A-A) represents Chess Set # 3. Chess Set # 1 positions similarly to the conventional (G-G) VERTICAL position arrangement, at the Bottom (Ground) Platform level and Chess Set # 2 arrangement is the (G-G) HORIZONTAL position arrangement also at the Bottom (Ground) Platform level. Furthermore, Chess Set # 3 arrangement resembles the conventional (A-A) VERTICAL initial position display.

Photo 21 examines a possible GROUND-TO-AIR/GROUND-TO-GROUND/AIR-TO-AIR (G-A)/(G-G)/(A-A) initial position setup for a Triple Set game. Chess Set # 1, represented by the first Group of letters (G-A) is VERTICAL, Non-uniform (because Player I Orange-Blue color band White chess pieces position at the Bottom (Ground) level whereas Player II Black chess pieces station at the Top (Air) level, non-Linear chess game. Chess Set # 2, represented by the second Group of letters (G-G) is a HORIZONTAL, Uniform (because BOTH chess sets for Player I and Player II are at the Bottom (Ground) level), Non-Linear chess game. Chess Set #3, represented by the third Group of letters (A-A) resemble a conventional VERTICAL (initial position display), Uniform (because Player I and Player II chess pieces locate at the Top (Air) level), non-Linear chess game.

Photo 22 explains a possible position scenario for a GROUND-TO-AIR/GROUND-TO-AIR/AIR-TO-GROUND (G-A)/(G-A)/(A-G) initial position setup for a Triple Set game. Chess Set # 1,represented by the first Group of letters (G-A) is a VERTICAL, Non-Uniform(because Player I chess pieces locate at the Lower Bottom (L.B.) section of the Bottom (Ground) Platform and Player II chess pieces situate at the Upper Top (U.T.) section of the Top (Air) Platform), non-Linear Chess game.

Photo 23 reveals a possible position scenario for an AIR-TO-GROUND/AIR-TO-GROUND/GROUND-TO-AIR (A-G)/(A-G)/(G-A) initial position setup for a Triple Set game. Chess Set # 1 represented by the first Group of letters (A-G) resembles an initial position arrangement similar to a VERTICAL, Non-Uniform (because Player I Orange-Blue color band White chess pieces locate at the Lower Top (L.T.) section, Base (1) of the Top (Air) Platform and Player II Black pieces situates at the Upper Bottom (U.B.) section, Base (0) of the Bottom (Ground) Platform), non-Linear chess game.

Photo 24 discusses a possible position scenario for an AIR-TO-AIR/AIR-TO-AIR/GROUND-TO-GROUND (A-A)/(A-A)/(G-G) initial position setup for a Triple Set game. Chess Set # 1 represented by the first Group of letters (A-A) shows a VERTICAL, Uniform (because Player I Orange-Blue color band White chess pieces positions at the Lower Top (L.T.) section, Base(1) of the Top (Air) Platform and Player II Black chess pieces station at the Upper Top (U.T.) section, Base (1) also at the Top Platform), Non-Linear chess game. Chess Set # 2 represented by the second Group of letters (A-A) displays a HORIZONTAL, Uniform (because Player I Orange-Red color band Black chess pieces locates at the Top Left (T.L.) section, Base (1) of the Top (Air) Platform and Player II White chess pieces situates at the Top Right (T.R.) section, Base (1) also at the Top (Air) Platform), non-Linear chess game. Chess Set # 3 represented by the third Group of letters (G-G) indicates a VERTICAL, Uniform(because Player I Red-Purple color band White chess pieces position at the Lower Bottom (L.B.) section, Base (0) of the

Bottom (Ground) Platform and Player II Black chess pieces station at the Upper Bottom (U.B.) section, Base (0) also at the Bottom (Ground) Platform), non-Linear chess game.

Photo 25 presents a possible position scenario for an AIR-TO-GROUND/GROUND-TO-GROUND/AIR-TO-AIR (A-G)/(G-G)/(A-A) initial position setup for a Triple Set game. Chess Set # 1 represented by the first Group of letters (A-G) displays a VERTICAL, Non-uniform (because Player I Orange-Blue color band White chess pieces position at the Lower Top (L.T.) section, Base (1) of the Top (Air) Platform and Player II Black pieces station at the Upper Bottom(U.B.) section, Base (0) of the Bottom (Ground) Platform) chess game. Chess Set # 2 indicated by the second Group of letters (G-G) reveals a HORIZONTAL, Uniform (because Player I Orange-Red color band Black chess pieces position at the Bottom Left (B.L.) section, Base (0) of the Bottom (Ground) Platform and Player II White chess pieces station at the Bottom Right (B.R.) section, Base (0) also at the Bottom (Ground) Platform), non-Linear chess game. Chess Set # 3, presented by the third Group of letters (A-A) reveals a HORIZONTAL, Uniform (because Player I Red-Purple color band White chess pieces position at the Top Left (T.L.) section, Base (1) of the Top (Air) Platform and Player II Black chess pieces station at the Top Right (T.R.) section, Base (1) also at the Top (Air) Platform), non-Linear chess game.

****

Abbreviations of the Hexagonal Platforms

L.B. (0) = Lower Bottom Platform at the Bottom Level of Base (0).
U.B. (0) = Upper Bottom Platform at the Bottom Level of Base (0).
B.L. (0) = Bottom Left Platform at the Bottom Level of Base (0).
B.R. (0) = Bottom Right Platform at the Bottom Level of Base (0).
B.C. (0) = Bottom Center Level at the Bottom Level of Base (0).
T.C. (1) = Top Center Level at the Top Level of Base (1).
L.T. (1) = Lower Top Platform at the Top Level of Base (1).
U.T. (1) = Upper Top Platform at the Top Level of base (1).
T.L. (1) = Top Left Platform at the Top Level of Base (1).
T.R. (I) = Top Right Platform at the Top Level of Base (1).

****

Included in this Advanced Chess Book are these Greek Symbols:

Alpha = α
Beta = β
Gamma = γ
Sigma = σ

****

Alpha Prime = α'
Beta Prime = β'
Gamma Prime = γ'
Sigma Prime = σ'

SECTION A
PHOTOS AND DIAGRAMS

"Photo 7 -Single Set Game Having a GROUND-TO-GROUND(G-G)
Set-Up Configuration."

"Photo - Orange-Blue color band chess pieces. The circular color band kit is included with the chess
game. The color band(s) needs to be twisted and turned onto the chess pieces to fit both at the top and
bottom of the chess piece; a snug fit is appropriate so as not to overstretch the color bands which will
result in the breakage of the band."

**"Photo 8 - Single Set Game Showing The GROUND-TO-AIR(G-A)
Initial Set-Up Configuration."**

"Photo 9 - Single Set Game-AIR-TO-AIR (A-A) Initial Set-Up Configuration."

"Photo 10 - Single Set Game-AIR-TO-GROUND(A-G) Initial Set-Up."

"Photo 11 - Single Set Game GROUND-TO-AIR (G -A) Initial Set-Up."

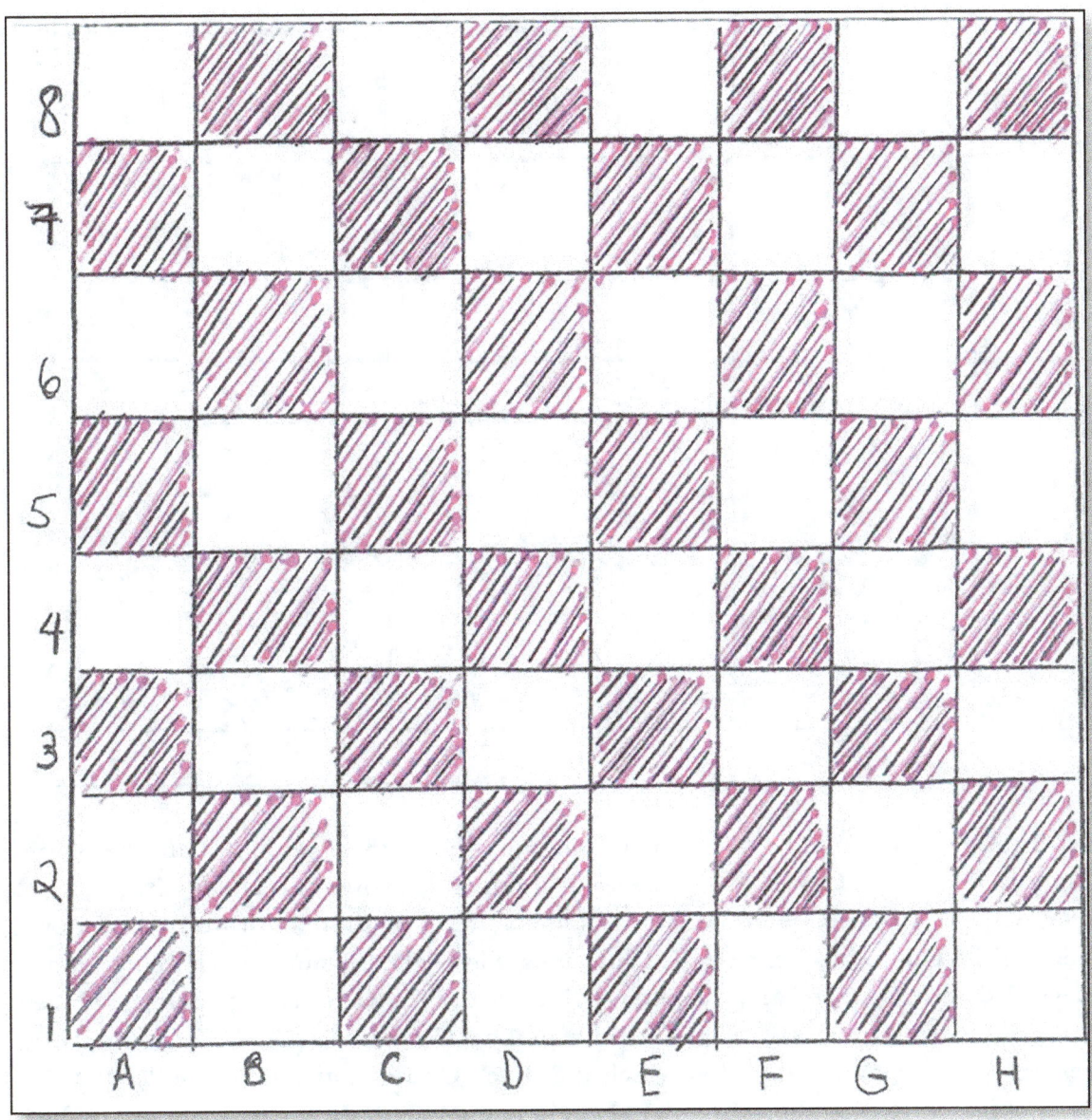

"Diagram 1 (original book page # 57). This diagram shows a Conventional Chess board. The enumeration of the Rows is from numbers 1-8 starting at the Bottom Row #1 and ascending to the Top Row #8. The Column label starts with the letter "A" at the extreme left of the board and ends with the letter "G" at the extreme right of the board."

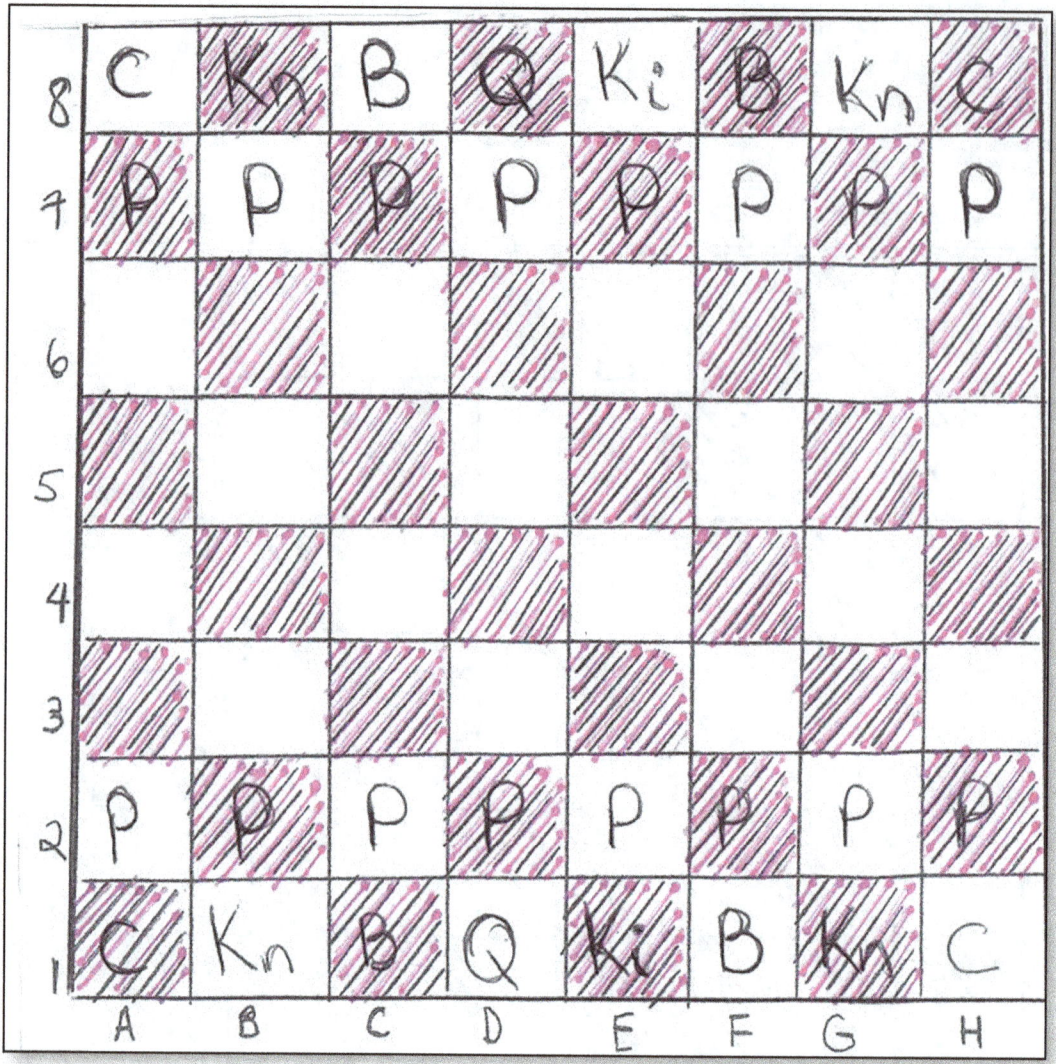

"Diagram 2 (original book page # 58): This diagram shows the position of the chess pieces on a Conventional Chess board. Player I white pieces position on the squares that constitute both Row 1 and Row 2. Player II black pieces station on all the squares that constitute both Row 7 and Row 8. Notice that Player I White Queen positions on the white square at Q 1D; the number "1" represents the Row at which Player I Queen positions and the letter "D" indicates the Column at which the Queen situates. Player II Black Queen stations at the opposite side of the game board at Q 8D; for Player II the number "8" represents the Row on the Board at which the Black Queen stations and the letter "D" indicates the Column of its location on the conventional chess game board. Please note that an A Queen always positions on the square of its color during the initial set-up at the start of a game. For example, a white Queen must position on the white square at the start of the game and likewise a black Queen should station on the black square at the initial start of the game."

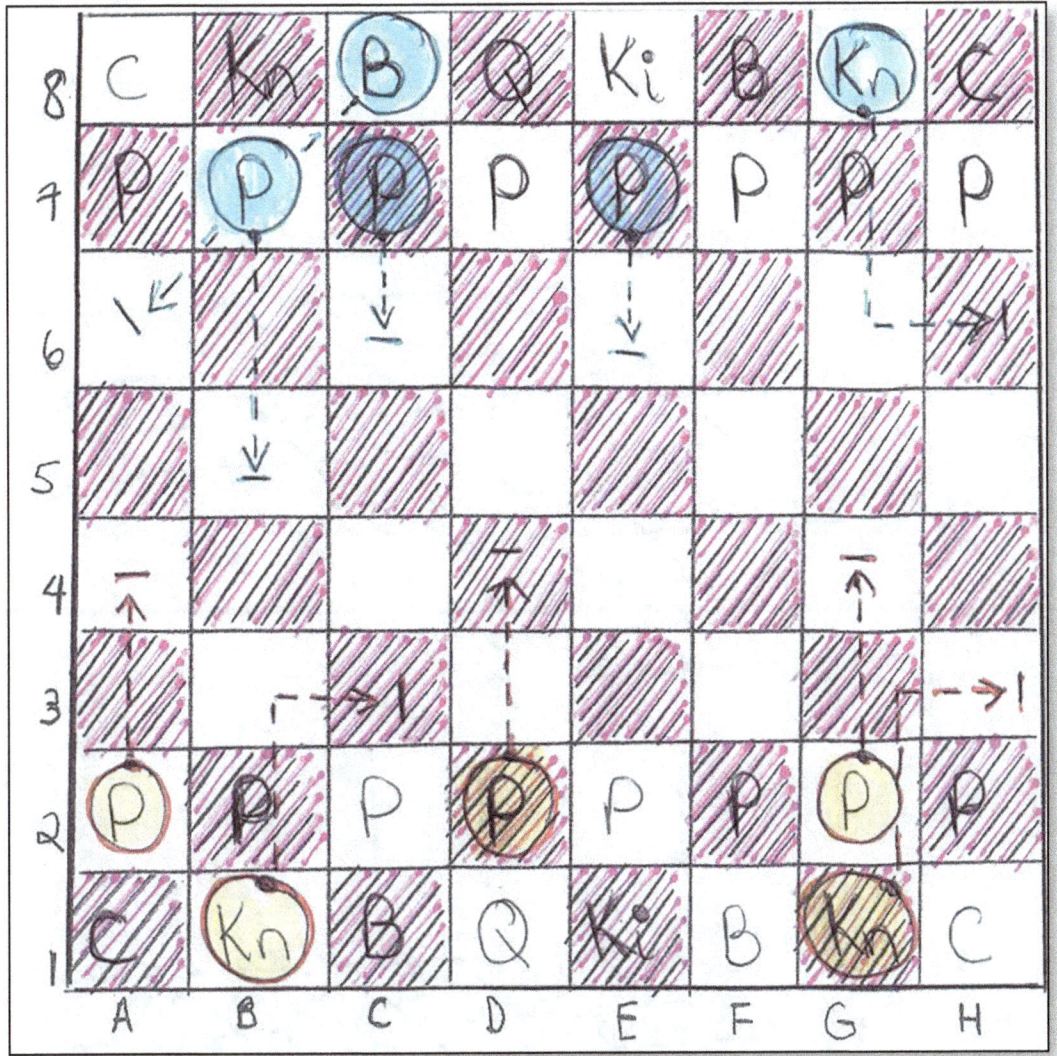

"Diagram 3 (original book page # 59): This diagram depicts the initial Movements of the chess pieces of a Single Set game on a conventional game board. The Yellow color shade indicates Player I chess piece movements. The Blue color shade depicts Player II chess piece movements. The letter "Kn" represents the Knights; the movement of the Knight displaces in a 3/2 squares Forward Advance movement. The letter "B" stands for the Bishops; this piece moves diagonally across the game board. The letter "Q" indicates the Queens and the letter "Ki" represents the Kings. The objective of the game is to capture or remove an opponent's King."

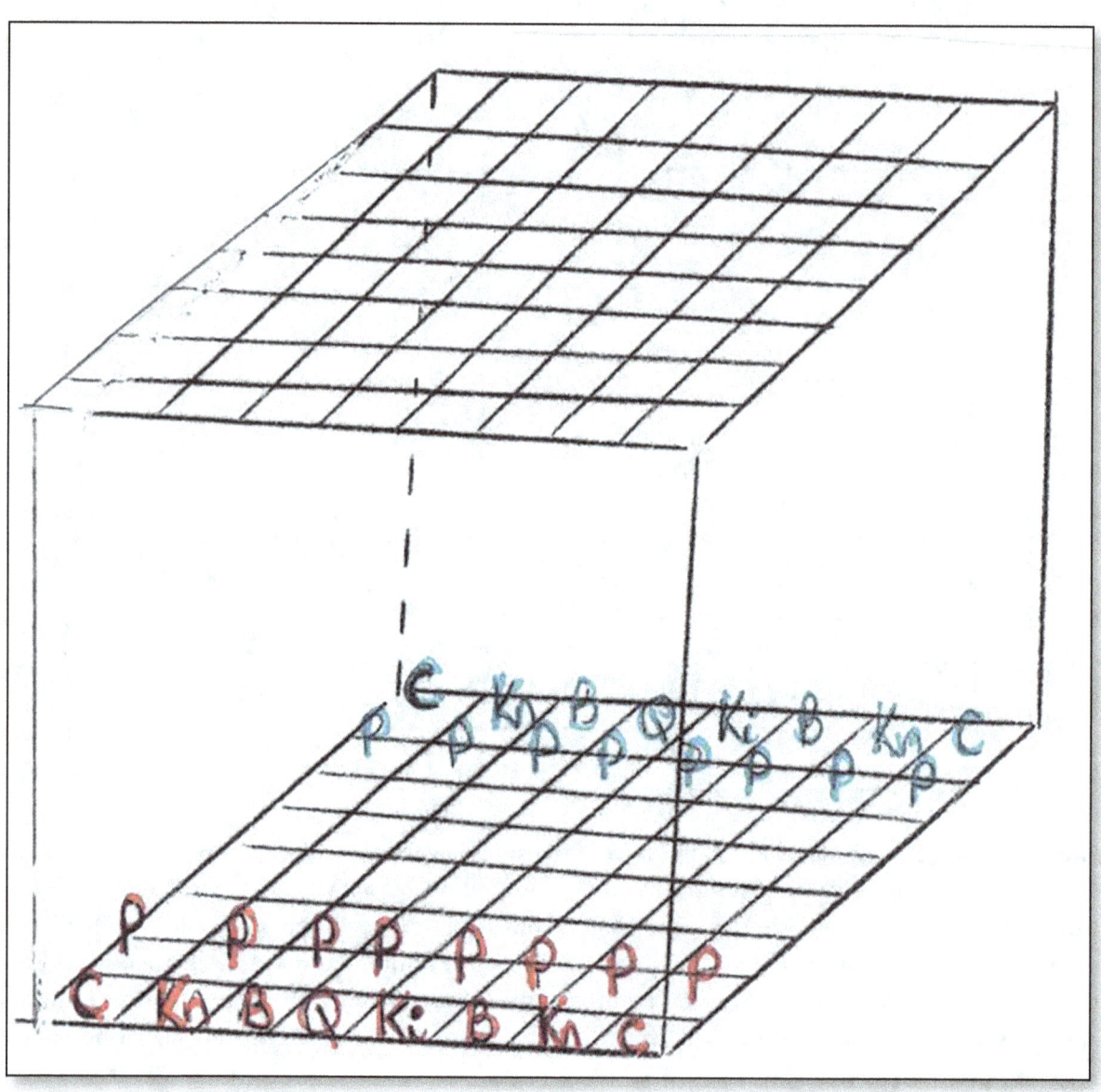

"Diagram 4 (original book page # 63): This diagram depicts the Cubic game board of a Single Set chess game having double-layer Platforms. The Bottom layer is the GROUND Platform, and the Top layer is the AIR. The initial position set-up configuration for this Single Set game is "GROUND-TO-GROUND" which shows symbolically as (G-G). The chess piece movements may occur at both layers sporadically and intermittently."

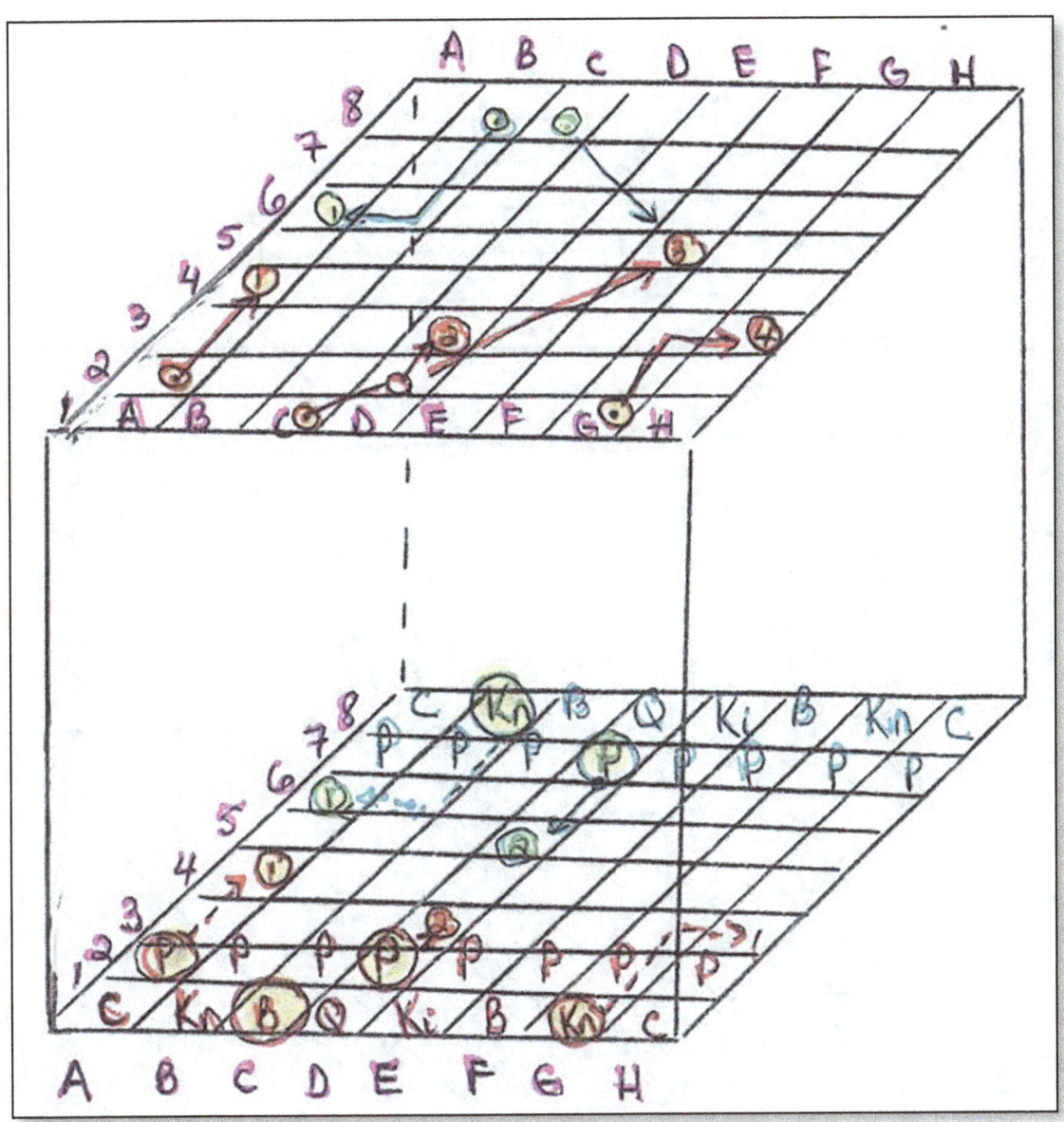

"Diagram 5 (original book page # 65): Presents the initial chess movements of a Single Set game on the Cubic game boards. The game has a (G-G) initial set-up configuration. The color shade indicates the chess piece movements."

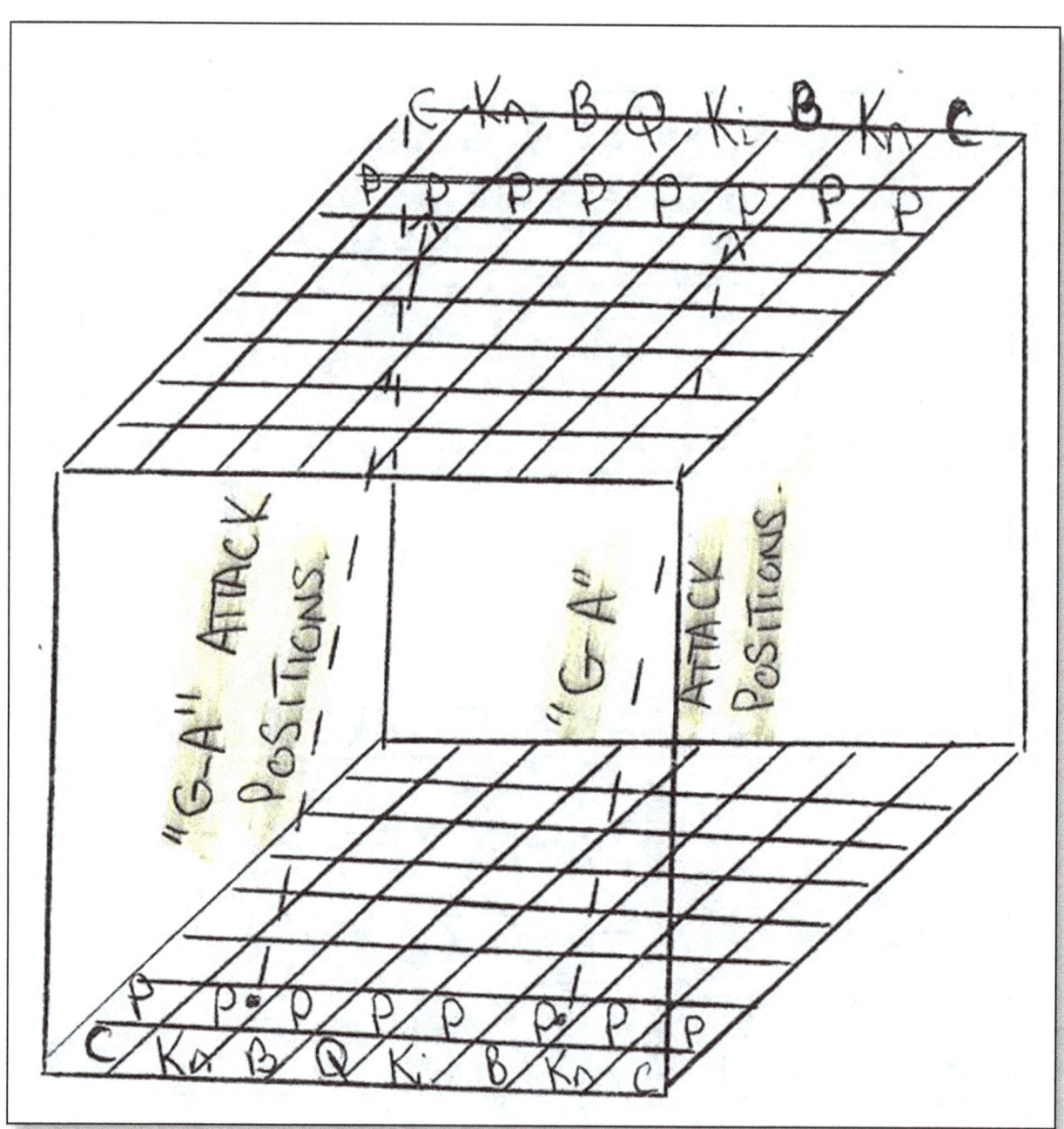

"Diagram 6 (original book page # 75): This diagram presents a Cubic game with a Single Set display having a "GROUND-TO-AIR" (G-A) initial set-up position configuration. Player I pieces position at the Bottom (GROUND) level and Player II pieces station at the Top (AIR) level. This game is a Non-Uniform, Linear Single Set game; the game is non-Uniform since it starts on double-layer Platforms."

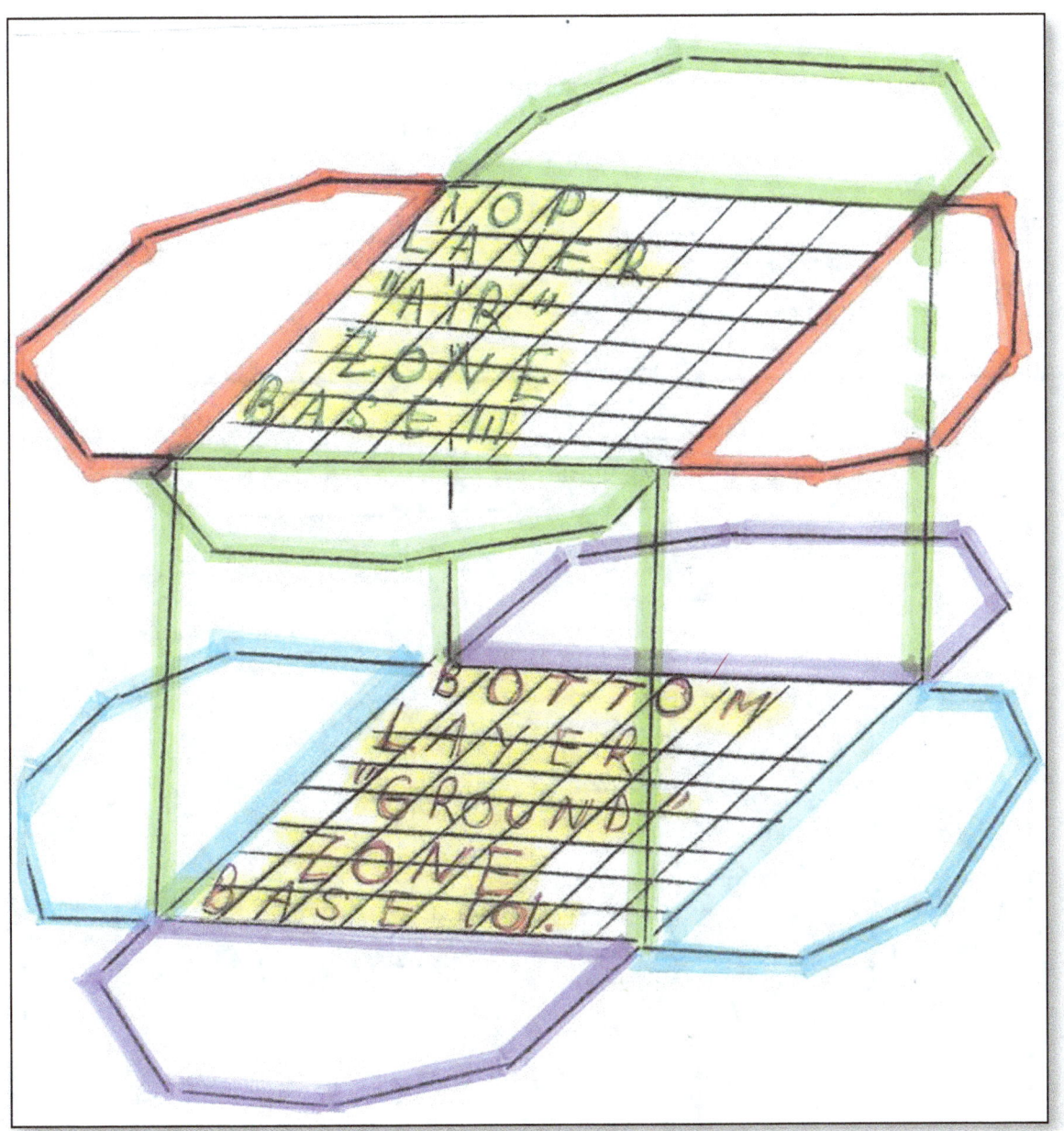

The handwritten text within the image reads:

TOP
LAYER
"AIR"
ZONE
BASE (1)

BOTTOM
LAYER
"GROUND"
ZONE
BASE (0)

"Diagram 7 (original book page # 8): This diagram depicts the layers of the Latitudinal Star Gate 14 model. The Bottom (GROUND) layer designates as Base (0) and the Top (AIR) layer designates as Base (1). The Center grid of the Bottom layer is the Bottom Center which symbolically shows as (B.C.) at Base (0). The Center grid of the Top layer is the Top Center which symbolically indicates as (T.C.) at Base (1)."

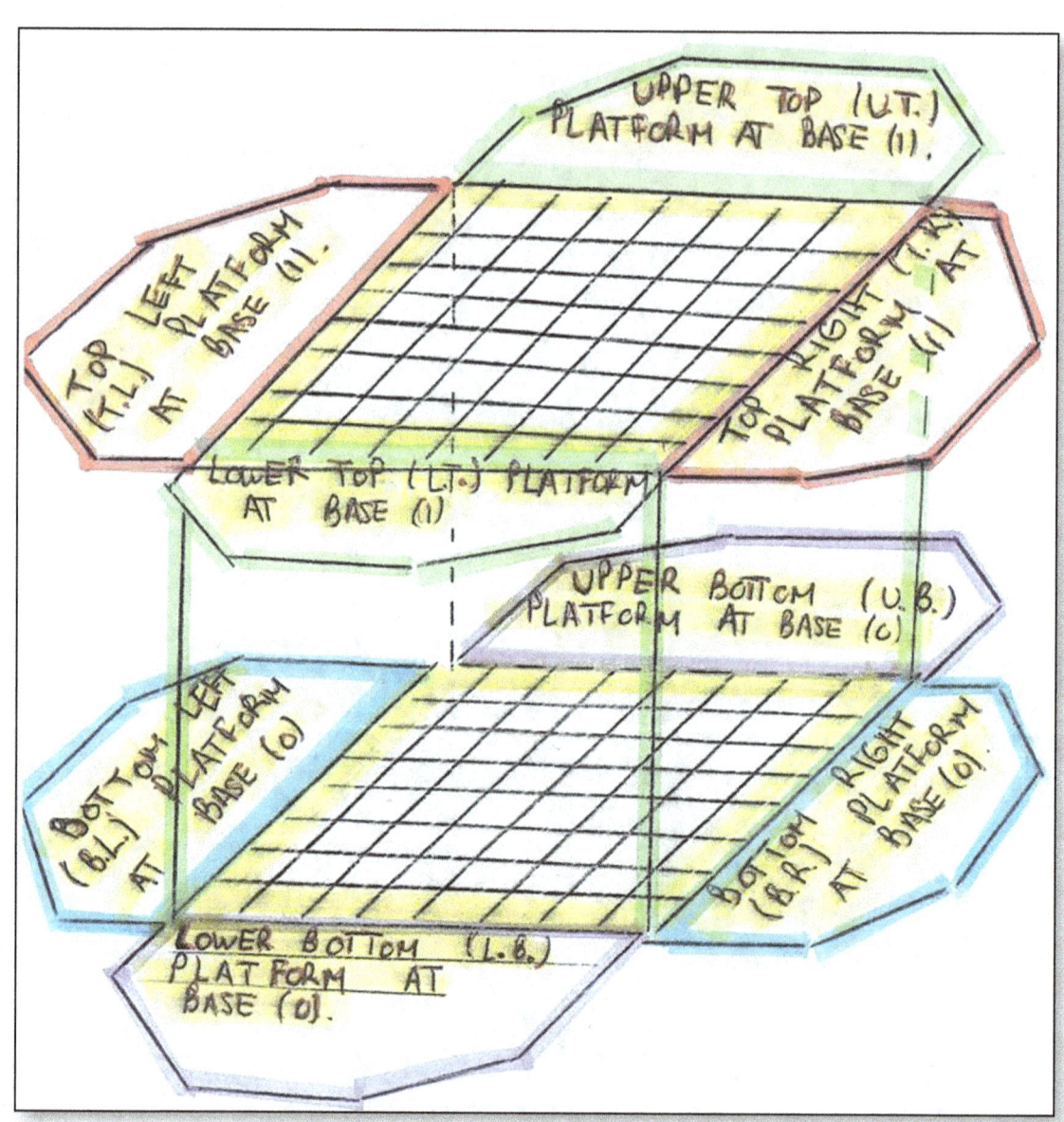

"Diagram 8 (original book page # 9): This diagram names the various Sections of the Bottom Platform and the Top Platform of the Latitudinal S.G.14 model."

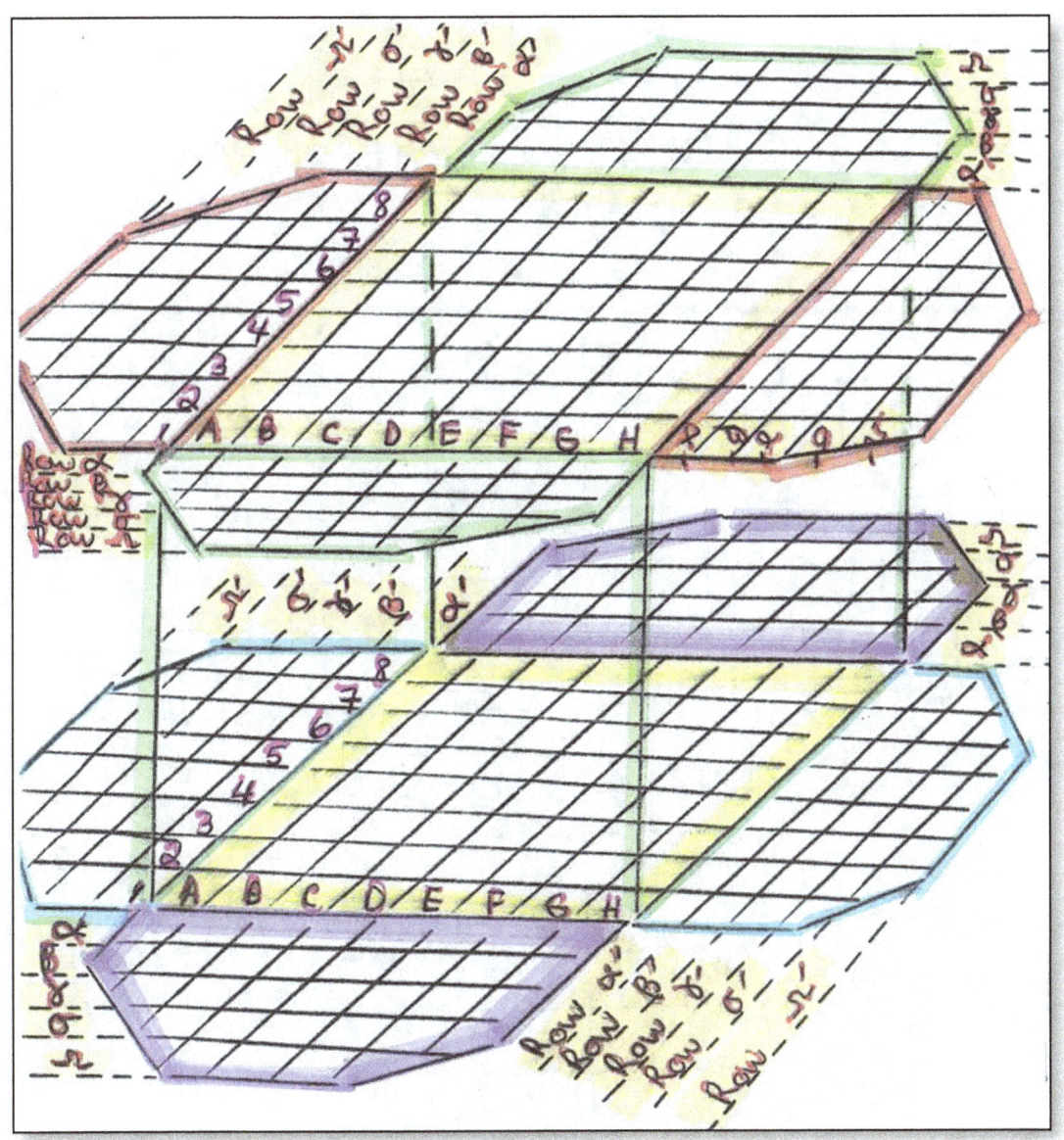

"Diagram 9 (original book page # 10): This illustration displays the Coordinates of the Lat.S.G.14 model."

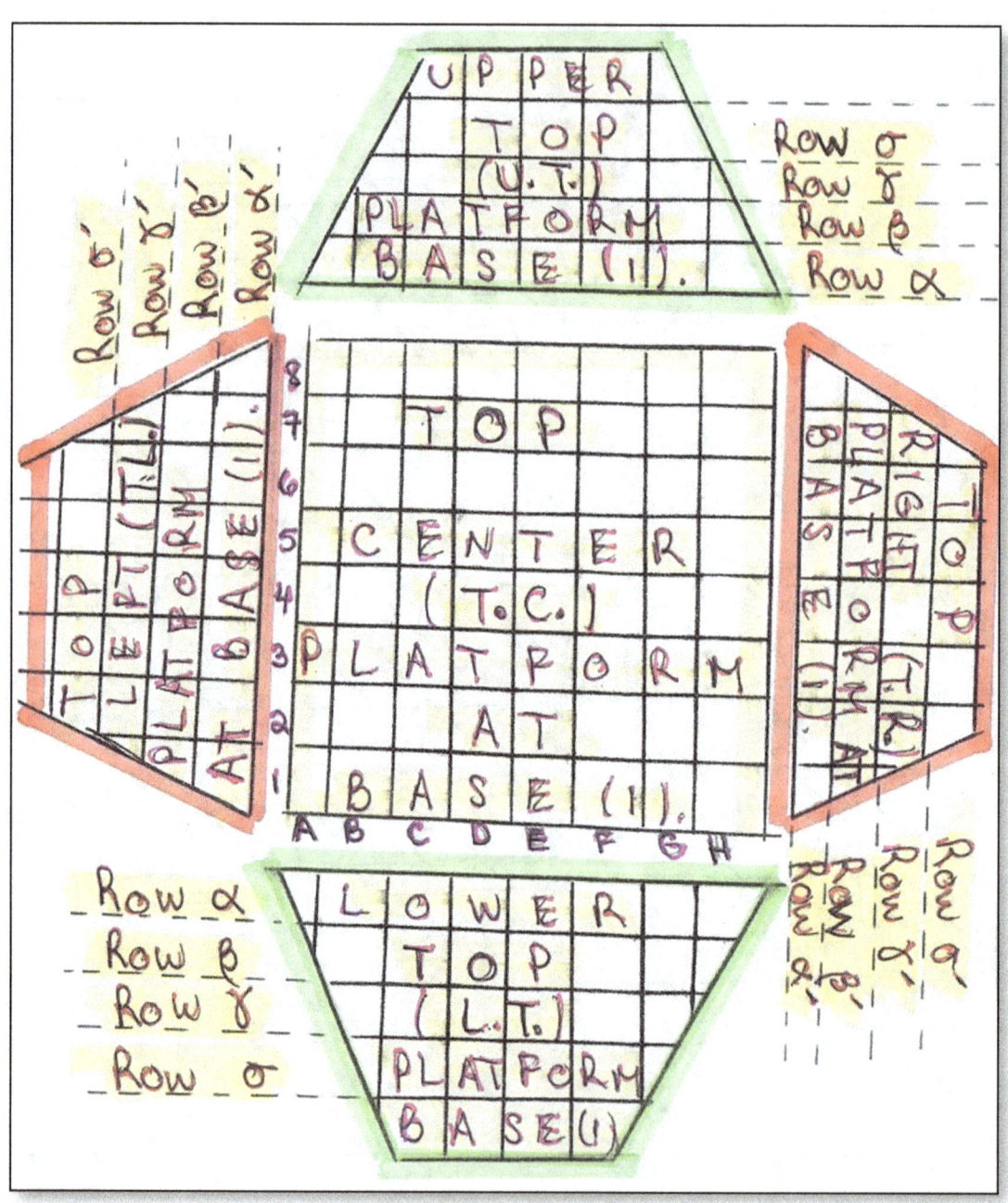

"Diagram 10 (original book page 19): This illustration shows the Sections and the Coordinates of the Top (AIR) Platform of the Long.S.G.14 model."

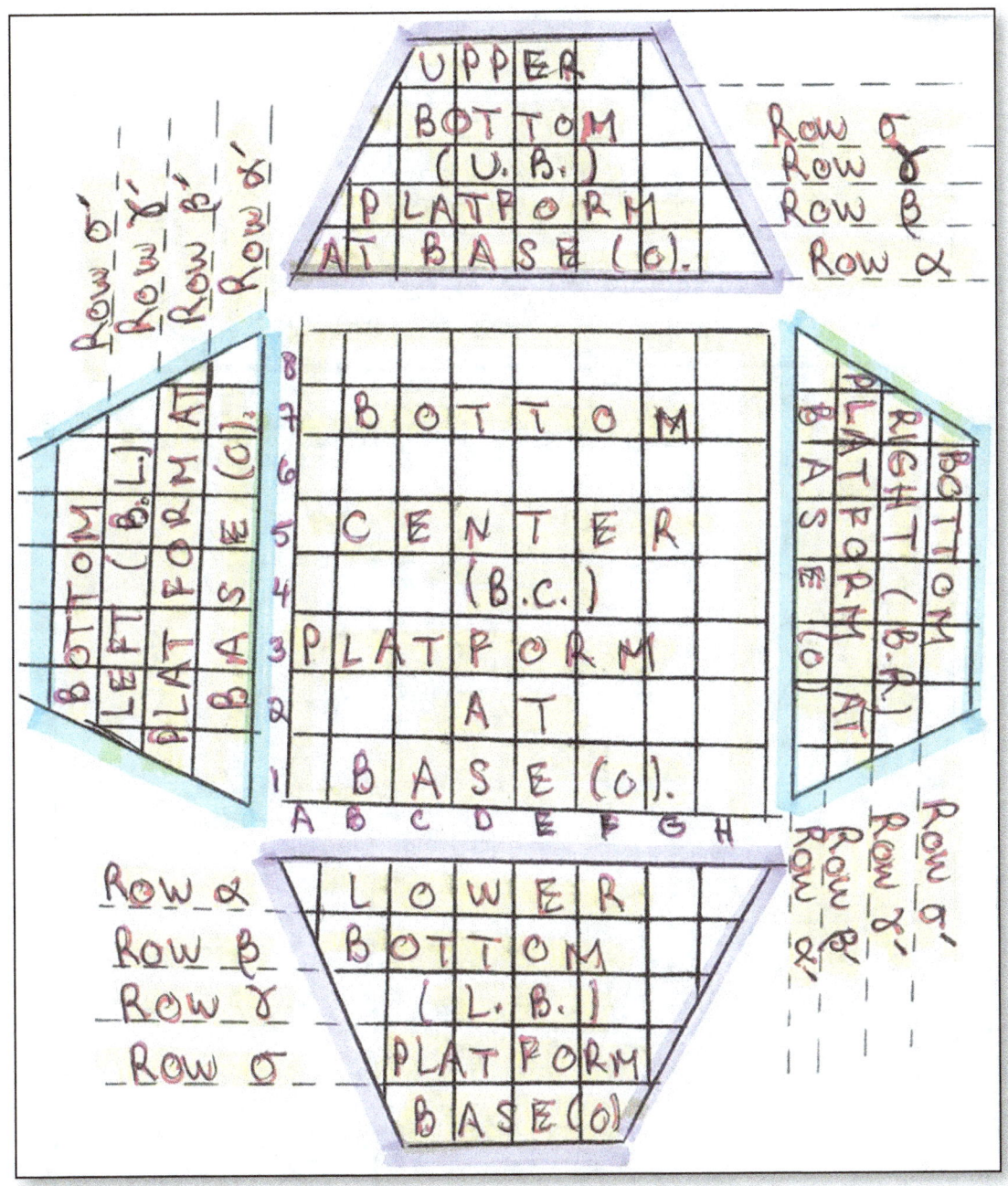

"Diagram 11 (original book page # 20): This drawing depicts the Sections and the Coordinates of the Bottom Platform of the Long.S.G.14 model."

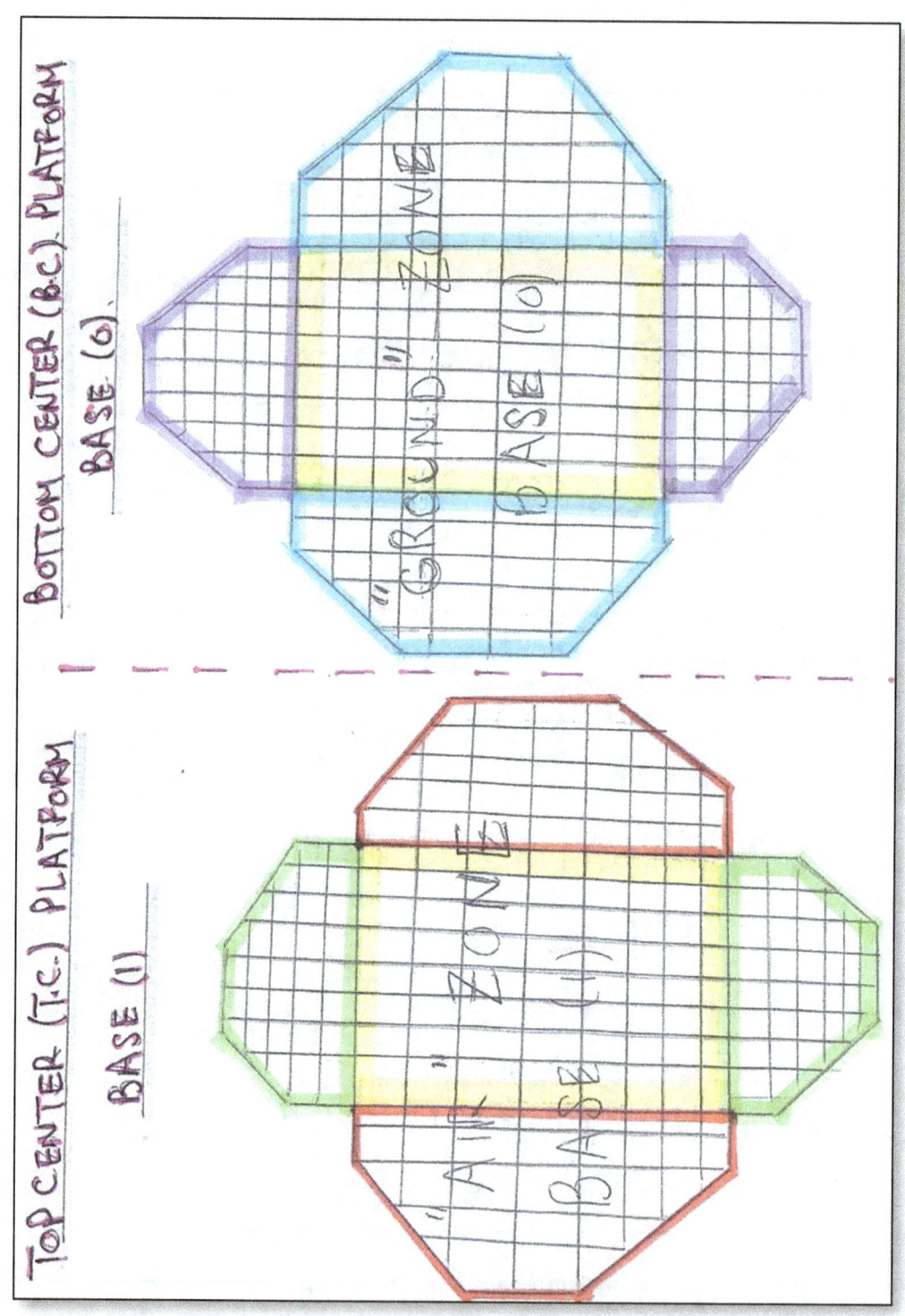

"Diagram 12 (original book page # 16): Names the two types of Platforms of the Long. S.G.14 model."

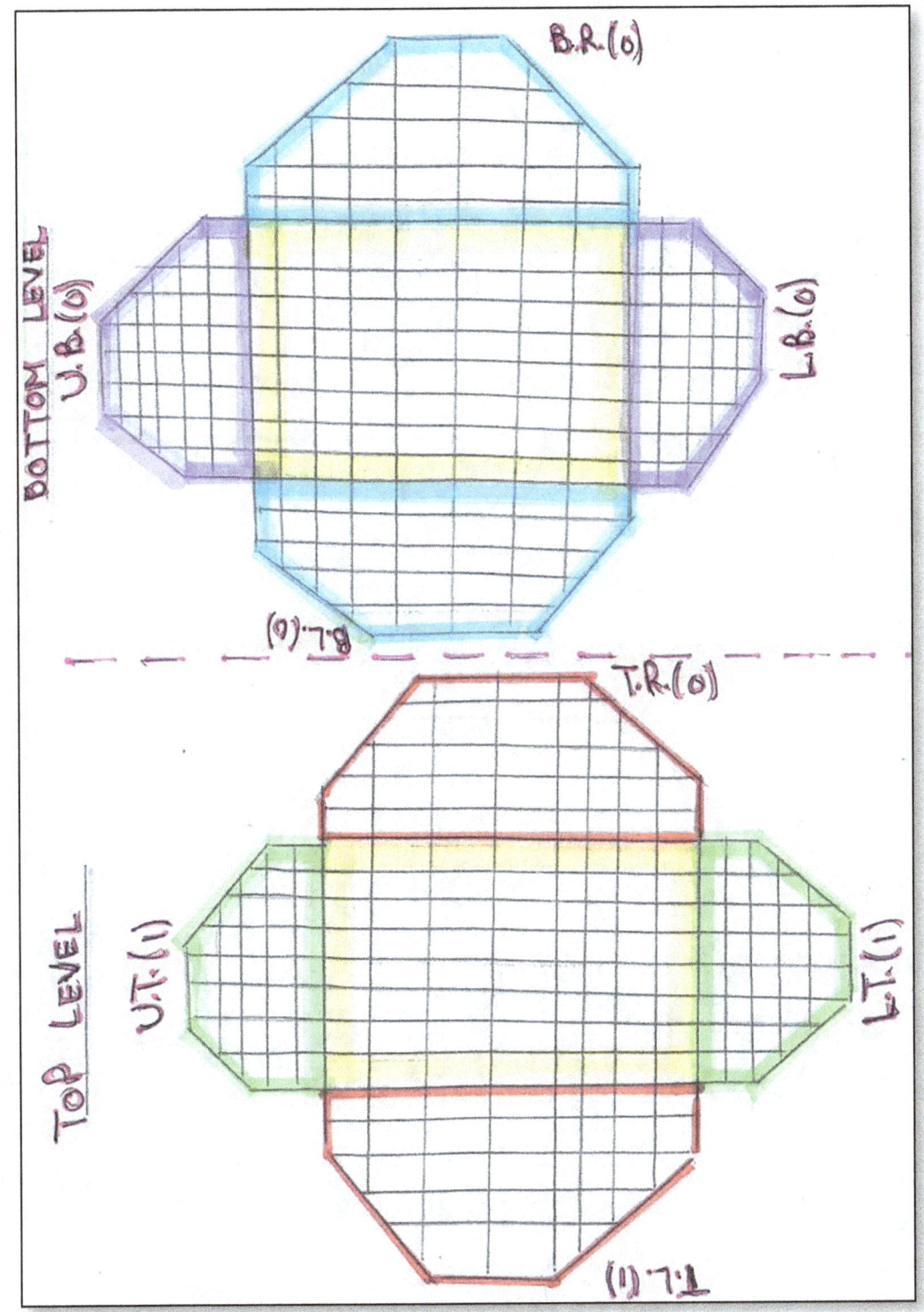

"Diagram 13 (original book page # 18): This diagram depicts the abbreviations for the Sections of the Long.S.G.14 model."

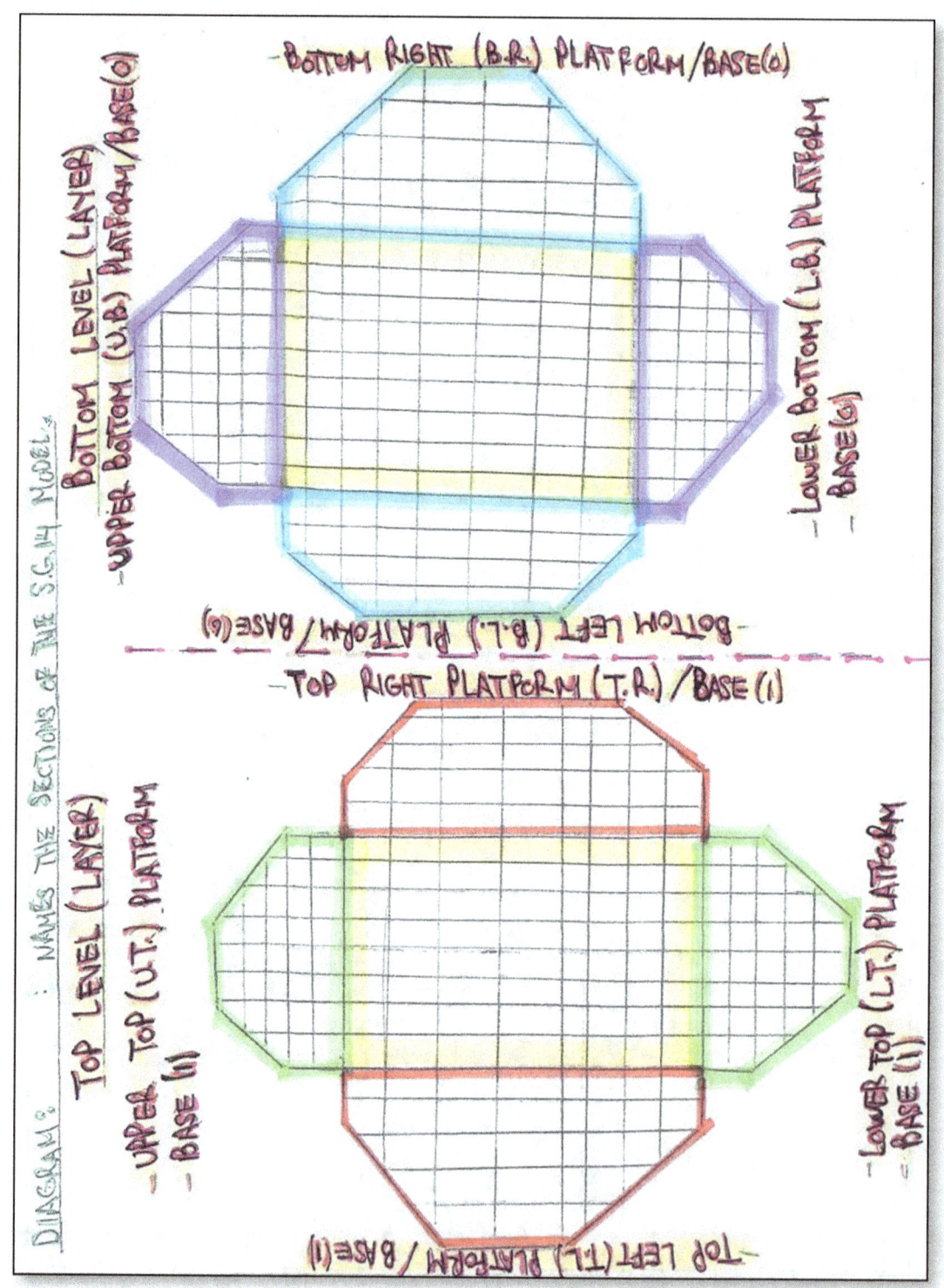

DIAGRAM: - NAMES THE SECTIONS OF THE S.G.14 MODEL.

BOTTOM LEVEL (LAYER)
-UPPER BOTTOM (U.B.) PLATFORM/BASE(o)

BOTTOM RIGHT (B.R.) PLATFORM/BASE(o)

- LOWER BOTTOM (L.B.) PLATFORM
- BASE(o)

-BOTTOM LEFT (B.L.) PLATFORM/BASE(o)

-TOP RIGHT PLATFORM (T.R.)/BASE (i)

TOP LEVEL (LAYER)
-UPPER TOP (U.T.) PLATFORM
- BASE (i)

-LOWER TOP (L.T.) PLATFORM
- BASE (i)

-TOP LEFT (T.L.) PLATFORM/BASE(i)

"Diagram 14 (original book page # 17): The Sections of the Long.S.G.14 model."

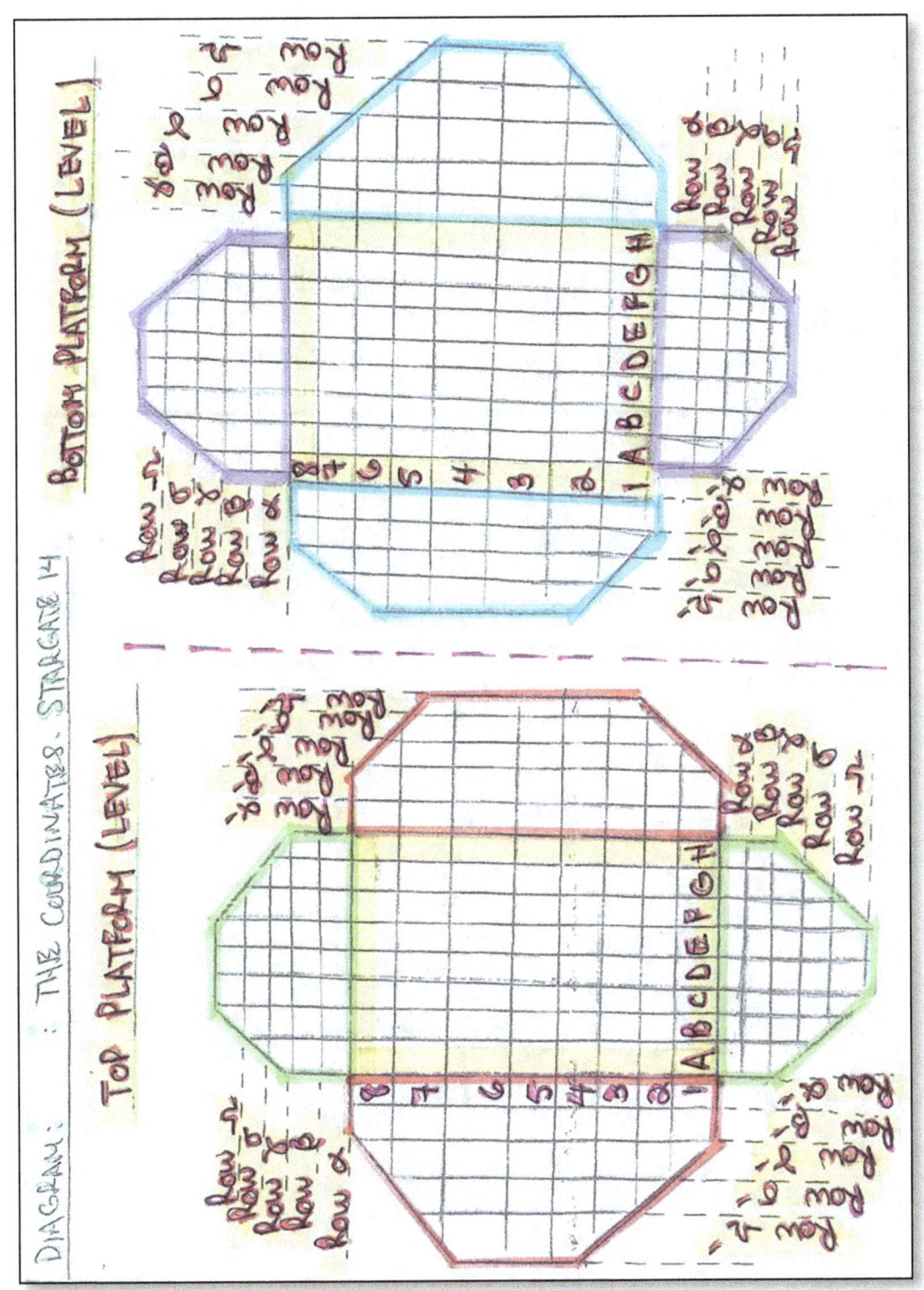

"Diagram 15 (original book page # 24): Displays the Coordinates of the Long.S.G.14 model."

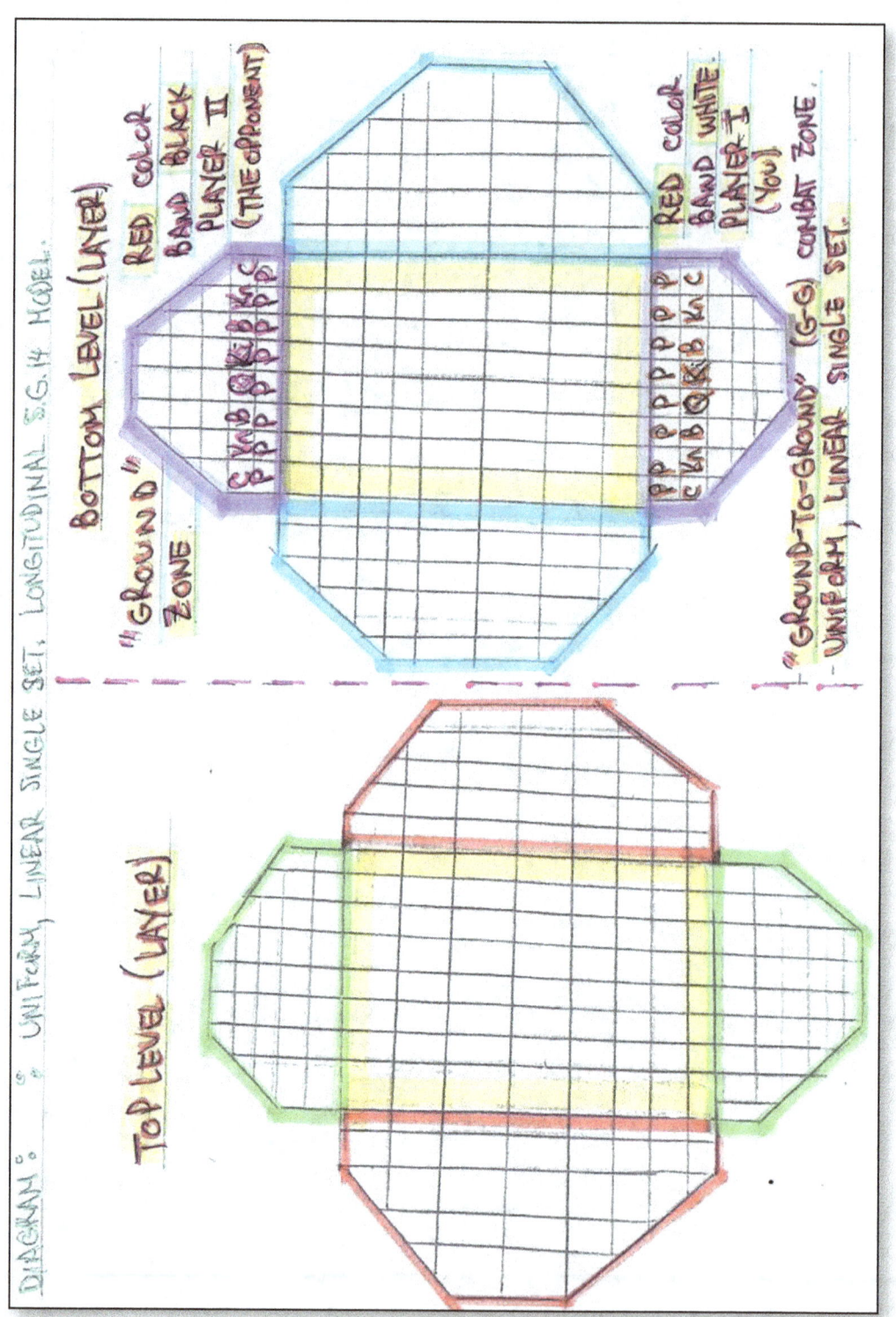

DIAGRAM : = UNIFORM, LINEAR SINGLE SET. LONGITUDINAL S.G.14 MODEL.

BOTTOM LEVEL (LAYER)

TOP LEVEL (LAYER)

RED COLOR BAND BLACK PLAYER II (THE OPPONENT)

RED COLOR BAND WHITE PLAYER I (YOU)

"GROUND" ZONE

"GROUND-TO-GROUND" (G-G) COMBAT ZONE. UNIFORM, LINEAR SINGLE SET.

"Diagram 16 (original book photo # 38): This diagram shows the GROUND-TO-GROUND initial position set-up configuration for a Single Set, Uniform, Linear chess game."

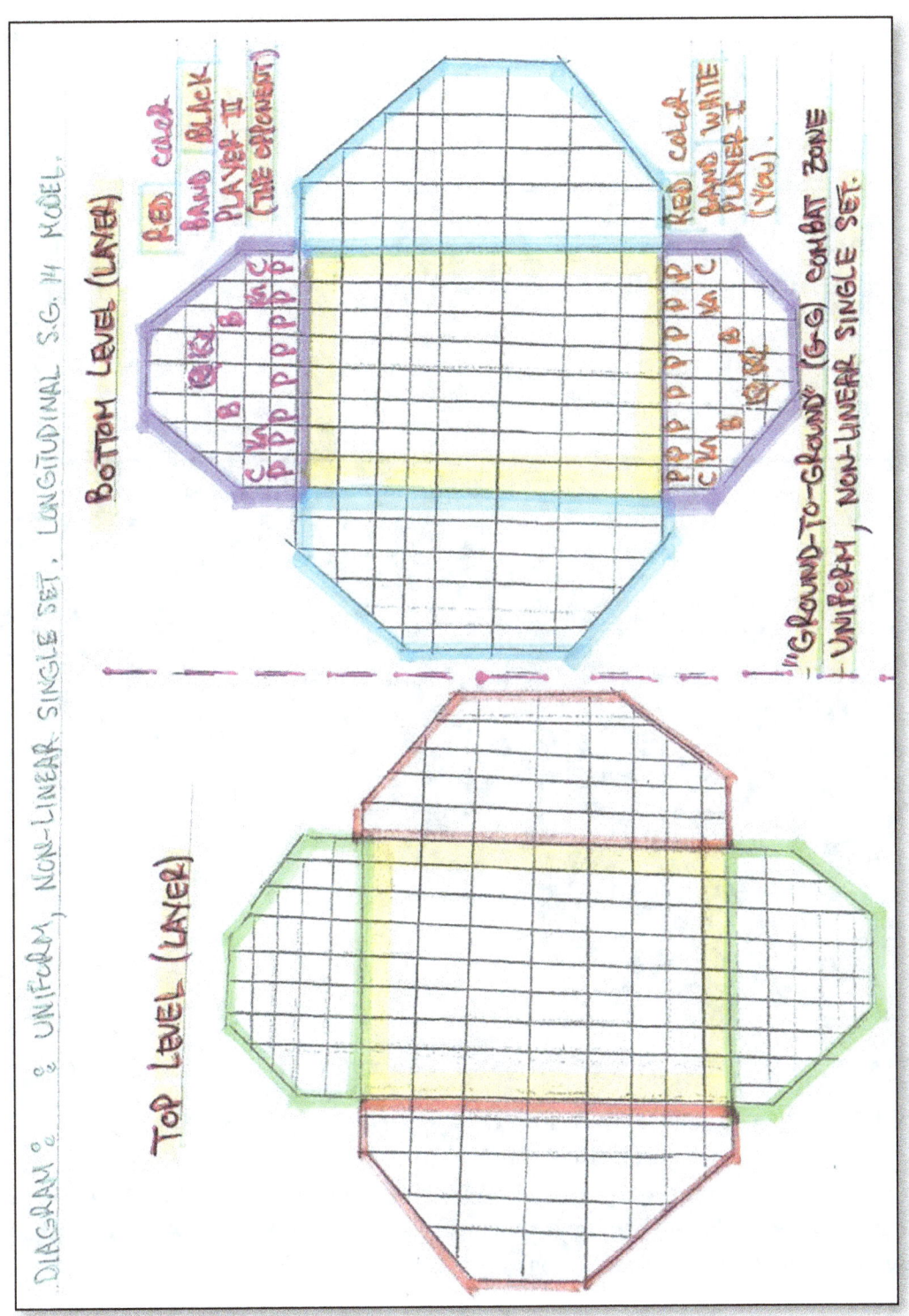

Diagram 17 - (original book page # 41): Unveils the initial GROUND-TO-GROUND (G-G) set-up position scenario for a Single Set, Uniform, Non-Linear chess game on the Longitudinal Star Gate 14 model.

Photo 7 - GROUND-TO-GROUND (G-G) Initial Set-Up. (Page 32). This photo presents the **GROUND-TO-GROUND(G-G)** initial set-up position configuration for a Single Set, Uniform, Non-Linear chess game. Player I control the Orange-Blue color band White pieces that position at the Lower Bottom (L.B.) section of the game board. Player II controls the Orange-Blue color band Black pieces that station at the Upper Bottom (U.B.) section of the game board.

Photo 8 - GROUND-TO-AIR (G-A) Initial Set-Up. (Page 33). This photo shows the GROUND-TO-AIR (G-A) initial position set-up. Player I Orange-Blue color band White chess pieces position at the Lower Bottom (L.B.) section of the Bottom (GROUND) Platform at Base (0). Player II Orange-Blue color band Black chess pieces station at the Upper Top (U.T.) section of the Top (AIR) Platform at Base (1)."

Photo 9 - AIR-TO-AIR (A-A) Initial Set-Up. (Page 34). The AIR-TO-AIR (A-A) initial position set-up configuration of a Single Set, Uniform, Non-Linear game on the Long.S.G.14 model. Player I Orange-Blue color band White chess pieces position at the Lower Top (L.T.) section of the game board at Base (1). Player II Orange-Blue color band chess pieces station at the Upper Top (U.T.) section of the game board also at Base (1)."

Photo 10 - AIR-TO-GROUND (A-G) Initial Set-Up. (Page 35). Shows a Single Set, Non-Uniform, Non-Linear game having an **AIR-TO-GROUND (A-G)** initial position set-up configuration. Player I Orange-Blue color band White chess pieces position at the Lower Top (L.T.) section of the game board. Player II Orange-Blue color band Black chess pieces station at the Upper Bottom (U.B.) section of the game board.

Photo 11 -GROUND-TO-GROUND/GROUND-TO-GROUND(G-G)/(G-G) initial position setup configuration for a Double Set Game. Chess set # 1 is the Orange-Blue color band set and Chess Set # 2 is the Orange-Red color band set. Player I control the Orange-Blue color band White pieces that position at the Lower Bottom (L.B.) section at Base (0) of the Bottom (Ground) Platform and Player II maintains the Orange-Blue color band Black pieces that station at the Upper Bottom (U.B.) section at Base (0) of the Bottom (Ground) Platform (uniform setup); chess set # 1 uses the (G-G) VERTICAL positioning movements. In addition, Player I control the Orange-Red color band Black pieces that position at the Bottom Left (B.L.) section at Base (0) of the Bottom Platform and Player II maintains the Orange-Red color band White pieces that station at the Bottom Right (B.R.) section also at Base (0) of the Bottom Platform (uniform setup); chess set # 2 uses the (G-G) HORIZONTAL Positioning movements.

Photo 13 -AIR-TO-GROUND/GROUND-TO-GROUND(A-G)/(G-G) initial position configuration setup for a Double Set Game. Chess set # 1 is the Orange-Blue color band set and Chess Set # 2 is the Orange-Red color band set. Regarding Chess Set # 1, Player I control the Orange-Blue color band White pieces that position at the Lower Top (L.T.) section, Base (1) of the Top (Air) Platform and Player II maintains the Orange-Blue color band Black pieces that station at the Upper Bottom (U.B.) section, Base (0) of the Bottom (Ground) Platform (non-uniform setup); chess set # 1 uses the (A-G) VERTICAL positioning movements. Concerning Chess Set # 2, Player I control the Orange-Red color band Black pieces that position at the Bottom Left (B.L.) section, Base (0) of the Bottom (Ground) Platform and Player II maintains the Orange - Red color band White pieces that station at the Bottom Right (B.R.) section, Base (0) of the Bottom (Ground) Platform (uniform setup); chess set # 2 uses the (G-G) HORIZONTAL positioning movements.

Photo 14 -AIR-TO-AIR/GROUND-TO-GROUND(A-A)/(G-G) initial position configuration setup for a Double Set Game. Chess Set # 1 is the Orange-Blue color band set and Chess Set # 2 is the Orange-Red color band set. Regarding Chess Set # 1, Player I control the Orange-Blue color band White pieces that position at the Lower Top (L.T.) section, Base (1) of the Top (Air) Platform and Player II maintains the Orange-Blue color band Black pieces that station at the Upper Top (U.T.) section, also Base (1) of the Top (Air) Platform (uniform setup); chess set # 1 uses the (A-A) VERTICAL positioning movements. Concerning Chess Set # 2, Player II maintains the Orange-Red color band Black pieces that position at the Bottom Left (B.L.) section, Base (0) of the Bottom (Ground) Platform and Player II maintains the Orange-Red color band White pieces that station at the Bottom Right (B.R.) section, Base (0) of the Bottom (Ground) Platform (uniform setup); chess set # 2 uses the (G-G) HORIZONTAL positioning movements.

Photo 15 -AIR-TO-AIR/AIR-TO-GROUND(A-A)/(A-G) initial position configuration setup for a Double Set Game. Chess Set # 1 is the Orange-Blue color band set and Chess Set # 2 is the Orange-Red color band set. Regarding Chess Set # 1, Player I control the Orange-Blue color band White pieces that position at the Lower Top (L.T.) section, Base (1) of the Top (Air) Platform and Player II maintains the Orange-Blue color band Black pieces that station at the Upper Top (U.T.) section, Base (1) of the Top (Air) Platform (uniform setup); chess set # 1 uses the (A-A) VERTICAL positioning movements. Concerning Chess Set # 2, Player I control the Orange-Red color band Black pieces that position at the Top Left (T.L.) section, Base (1) of the Top (Air) Platform and Player II maintains the Orange-Red color band White pieces that station at the Bottom Right (B.R.) section, Base (0) of the Bottom (Ground) Platform (non-uniform setup); chess set # 2 uses the (A-G) HORIZONTAL positioning movements.

Photo 16 - AIR-TO-AIR/AIR-TO-AIR (A-A)/(A-A) initial position configuration setup for a Double Set Game. Chess Set # 1 is the Orange-Blue color band set and Chess Set # 2 is the Orange-Red color band set. Regarding Chess Set # 1, Player I control the Orange-Blue color band White pieces that position at the Lower Top (L.T.) section, Base (1) of the Top (Air) Platform and Player II maintains the Orange-Blue color Black pieces that station at the Upper Top (U.T.) section, also Base (1) of the Top (Air) Platform (uniform setup); chess set # 1 uses the (A-A) VERTICAL positioning movements. Concerning Chess Set # 2, Player I control the Orange - Red color band Black pieces that position at the Top Left (T.L.) section, Base (1) of the Top (Air) Platform and Player II maintains the Orange - Red color band White pieces that station at the Top Right (T.R.) section, also Base (1) of the Top (Air) Platform (uniform setup); chess set # 2 uses the (A-A) HORIZONTAL positioning movements.

Photo 17 - GROUND-TO-AIR/AIR-TO-AIR(G-A)/(A-A) initial position configuration setup for a Double Set Game. Chess Set # 1 is the Orange-Blue color band set and Chess Set # 2 is the Orange-Red color band set. Regarding Chess Set # 1, Player I control the Orange-Blue color band White pieces that position at the Lower Bottom (L.B.) section, Base (0) of the Bottom (Ground) Platform and Player II maintains the Orange-Blue color band Black pieces that station at the Upper Top (U.T.) section, Base (1) of the Top (Air) Platform (non-uniform setup); chess set # 1 uses the (G-A) VERTICAL positioning movements. Concerning Chess Set # 2, Player I control the Orange-Red color band Black pieces that position at the Top Left (T.L.) section, Base (1) of the Top (Air) Platform and Player II maintains the Orange-Red color band White pieces that station at the Top Right (T.R.) section, Base (1) of the Top (Air) Platform (uniform setup); chess set # 2 uses the (A-A) HORIZONTAL positioning movements.

Photo 18 -GROUND-TO-GROUND/AIR-TO-AIR(G-G)/(A-A) initial position configuration setup for a Double Set Game. Chess Set # 1 is the Orange-Blue color band set and Chess Set # 2 is the Orange-Red color band set. Regarding Chess Set # 1, Player I control the Orange-Blue color band pieces that positions at the Lower Bottom (L.B.) section, Base (0) of the Bottom (Ground) Platform and Player II maintains the Orange-Blue color band Black pieces that stations at the Upper Bottom (U.B.) section, Base (0) of the Bottom (Ground) Platform (uniform setup); chess set # 1 uses the (G-G) VERTICAL positioning movements. Concerning Chess Set # 2, Player I control the Orange-Red color band Black pieces that position at the Top Left (T.L.) section, Base (1) of the Top (Air) Platform and Player II maintains the Orange-Red color band White pieces that station at the Top Right (T.R.) section, Base (1) of the Top (Air) Platform (uniform setup); chess set # 2 uses the (A-A) HORIZONTAL positioning movements.

Photo 19 - GROUND-TO-GROUND/GROUND-TO-AIR(G-G)/(G-A) initial position configuration setup for a Double Set Game. Chess Set # 1 is the Orange-Blue color band set and Chess Set # 2 is the Orange-Red color band set. Regarding Chess Set # 1, Player I control the Orange-Blue color band White pieces that position at the Lower Bottom (L.B.) section, Base (0) of the Bottom (Ground) Platform and Player II maintains the Orange-Blue color band Black pieces that station at the Upper Bottom (U.B.) section, Base (0) of the Bottom (Ground) Platform (uniform setup); chess set # 1 uses the (G-G) VERTICAL positioning movements. Concerning Chess Set # 2, Player I control the Orange-Red color band Black pieces that position at the Bottom Left (B.L.) section, Base (0) of the Bottom (Ground) Platform and Player II maintains the Orange-Red color band White pieces that stations at the Top Right (T.R.) section, Base (1) of the Top (Air) Platform (non-uniform setup); chess set # 2 uses the (G-A) HORIZONTAL positioning movements.

Photo 20/ #8218 – GROUND-TO-GROUND/GROUND-TO-GROUND/AIR-TO-AIR(G-G)/(G-G)/(A-A) – indicates a possible initial position configuration set-up for a Triple Set Game. Chess Set # 1 is the Orange-Blue color band set represented by the first group of letters (G-G), Chess Set # 2 is the Orange-Red color band set represented by the second group of letters(G-G) and Chess Set # 3 is the Red-Purple color band set represented by the third group of letters (A-A). Regarding Chess Set # 1, Player I controls the Orange-Blue color band White pieces that position at the Lower Bottom(L.B.) section, Base(0) of the Bottom(Ground) Platform and Player II maintains the Orange-Blue color band Black pieces that station at the Upper Bottom(U.B.) section, Base(0) of the Bottom Platform. In regards to Chess Set # 2, Player I controls the Orange-Red color band Black pieces that position at the Bottom Left (B. L.) section, Base(0) of the Bottom Platform and Player II maintains the Orange-Red color band White pieces that station at the Bottom Right(B.R.) section, Base(0) also of the Bottom Platform. Concerning Chess Set # 3, Player I controls the Red-Purple color band White pieces that position at the Lower Top(L.T.) section, Base (1) of the Top(Air) Platform and Player II maintains the Red-Purple color band Black pieces that station at the Upper Top(U.T.) section, Base(1) also of the Top Platform. Furthermore, Chess Set # 1, which represents the first group of letters(G-G) uses the conventional VERTICAL movements for the pieces. Chess Set # 2, which represents the second group of letters(G-G) uses the HORIZONTAL movements for the pieces. Chess Set # 3, which represents the third group of letters (A-A) uses the VERTICAL movements for the pieces. Chess Set # 1 uses the conventional uniform position (since both Player I and Player II Orange-Blue color pieces initial position configuration are at the Bottom (Ground) Platform) for VERTICAL movements of the pieces. Chess Set # 2 uses the non-conventional, uniform position (since both Player I and Player II Orange-Red color band pieces initial position configuration are at the Bottom (Ground) Platform and moves HORIZONTALLY. Chess Set # 3 uses the conventional, uniform position (since both of Player I and Player II Red-Purple color band pieces initial position configuration are at the Top (Air) Platform) for conventional VERTICAL movements of the pieces.

Photo 21/# 8219 – GROUND-TO-AIR/GROUND-TO-GROUND/AIR-TO-AIR (G-A)/(G-G)/(A-A) – presents a possible initial position configuration for a Triple Set Game. Chess Set #1 is Orange-Blue color band set represented by the first group of letters(G-A), Chess Set #2 is Orange-Red color band set represented by the second group of letters (G-G) and Chess Set # 3 is the Red-Purple color band set represented by the third group of letters(A-A). Regarding Chess Set #1, Player I controls the Orange-Blue color band White pieces that position at the Lower Bottom (L.B.) section, Base(0) of the Bottom(Ground) Platform and Player II maintains the Orange-Blue color band Black pieces that station at the Upper Top (U.T.) section, Base(1) of the Top(Air) Platform. In regards to Chess Set # 2, Player I controls the Orange-Red color band Black pieces that position at the Bottom Left(B.L.) section, Base(0) of the Bottom Platform and Player II maintains the Orange-Red color band White pieces that station at Bottom Right (B.R.) section, Base(0) also of the Bottom Platform. Concerning Chess Set # 3, Player I controls the Red-Purple color band White pieces that position at the Top Right (T.R.) section, Base (1) of the Top (Air) Platform and Player II maintains the Red-Purple color band Black pieces that station at the Top Left (T.L.) section, Base(1) also of the Top Platform. Furthermore, Chess Set # 1 which represents the first group of letters (G-A) uses the non-uniform (since Player I Orange-Blue color band White pieces is at the Bottom (Ground) Platform and Player II Orange-Blue color band Black pieces rest on the Top (Air) Platform) VERTICAL movement for the pieces. In addition, Chess Set # 2 which represents the second group of letters (G-G) uses the non-conventional uniform position (since both of Player I and Player II Orange-Red color band pieces initial position configuration are at the Bottom Platform) for HORIZONTAL movement of the pieces. Similarly, Chess Set # 3 which represents the third group of letters (A-A) also uses the non-conventional uniform position (since both of Player I and Player II Red-Purple color band pieces initial position configuration are at the Top Platform) for HORIZONTAL movement of the pieces.

Photo 22/ # 8220 – GROUND-TO-AIR/GROUND-TO-AIR/AIR-TO-GROUND (G-A)/(G-A)/(A-G) – shows a possible initial position configuration for a Triple Set Game. Chess Set # 1 is the Orange-Blue color band set represented by the first group of letters (G-A), Chess Set # 2 is the Orange-Red color band set represented by the second group of letters(G-A) and Chess Set # 3 is the Red-Purple color band set represented by the third group of letters(A-G). Regarding Chess Set # 1, Player I controls the Orange-Blue color band White pieces that position at the Lower Bottom (L.B.) section, Base (0) of the Bottom (Ground) Platform and Player II maintains the Orange-Blue color band Black pieces that station at the Upper Top (U.T.) section, Base (1) of the Top (Air) Platform. With regards to Chess Set # 2, Player I control the Orange-Red color band Black pieces that position at the Bottom Left (B.L) section of the Bottom (Ground) Platform and Player II maintains the Orange-Red color band White pieces that station at the Top Right (T.R.) section of the Top (Air) Platform. Concerning Chess Set # 3, Player I control the Red-Purple color band White pieces the position at the Lower Top (L.T.) section of the Top Platform and Player II maintains the Red-Purple color band pieces that station at the Upper Bottom (U.B.) section of the Bottom Platform. Furthermore, Chess Set # 1 which represents the first group of letters (G-A) uses the conventional non-uniform position (since Player I Orange-Blue color band White pieces position at the Bottom (Ground) Platform and Player II Orange-Blue color band pieces rest at the Top (Air) Platform) for VERTICAL movement of the pieces. In addition, Chess Set # 2 which represents the second group of letters (G-A) uses the non-conventional, non-uniform position (since Player I Orange-Red color band Black pieces position at the Bottom (Ground) Platform and Player II Orange-Red color band White pieces station at the Top (Air) Platform) for HORIZONTAL movement of the pieces. Also, Chess Set # 3 which represents the third group of letters (A-G) uses the conventional, non-uniform position (since Player I Red-Purple color band White pieces position at the Top (Air) Platform and Player II Red-Purple color band Black pieces station at the Bottom (Ground) Platform) for VERTICAL movement for the pieces.

Photo 23/ # 8221 –AIR-TO-GROUND/AIR-TO-GROUND/GROUND-TO-AIR(A-G)/(A-G)/(G-A) – displays a possible initial position configuration for a Triple Set Game. Chess Set # 1 is the Orange-Blue color band set represented by the first group of letters (A-G), Chess Set # 2 is the Orange-Red color band set represented by the second group of letters (A-G) and Chess Set # 3 is the Red-Purple color band set represented by the third group of letters (G-A). With regards to Chess Set # 1, Player I controls the Orange-Blue color band White pieces that position at the Lower Top (L.T.) section, Base (1) of the Top (Air) Platform and Player II maintains the Orange-Blue color band Black pieces that station at the Upper Bottom (U.B.) section, Base (0) of the Bottom (Ground) Platform. Concerning Chess Set # 2 Player I controls the Orange-Red color band Black pieces that position at the Top Left (T.L.) section, Base (1) of the Top Platform and Player II maintains the Orange-Blue color band White pieces that station at the Bottom Right (B.R.) section, Base (0) of the Bottom Platform. With regards to Chess Set # 3, Player I controls the Red-Purple color band White pieces that position at the Lower Bottom (L.B.) section, Base (0) of the Bottom Platform and Player II maintains the Red-Purple color band Black pieces that station at the Upper Top (U.T.) section, Base (1) of the Top (Air) Platform. Chess Set # 1 uses the conventional, non-uniform position (Player I Orange-Blue color band White pieces position at the Top (Air) Platform and Player II Orange-Blue color band Black pieces station at the Bottom Platform) for VERTICAL movement of the pieces. Chess Set # 2 uses the non-convention, non-uniform position (Player I Orange-Red color band Black pieces position at the Top Platform and Player II Orange-Red color band White pieces station at the Bottom Platform) for the HORIZONTAL movement of the pieces. Chess Set # 3 uses the conventional, non-uniform position for VERTICAL movement of the pieces.

Photo 24/ # 8222 –AIR-TO-AIR/AIR-TO-AIR/GROUND-TO-GROUND(A-A)/(A-A)/(G-G) – illustrates a possible initial position configuration for a Triple Set Game. Chess Set # 1 is the Orange-Blue color band set represented by the first group of letters (A-A), Chess Set # 2 is the Orange-Red color band set represented by the second group of letters (A-A) and Chess Set # 3 is the Red-Purple color band set represented by the third group of letters (G-G). With regards to Chess Set # 1, Player I controls the Orange-Blue color band White pieces that position at the Lower Top (L.T.) section, Base (1) of the Top (Air) Platform and Player II maintains the Orange-Blue color band Black pieces that stations at the Upper Top (U.T.) section, Base (1) also of the Top Platform. Concerning Chess Set # 2, Player I controls the Orange-Red color band Black pieces that position at the Top Left (T.L.) section, Base (1) of the Top Platform and Player II maintains the Orange-Red color band White pieces that station at the Top Right (T.R.) section, Base (1) also of the Top Platform. In reference to Chess Set # 3, Player I controls the Red-Purple color band White pieces that position at the Lower Bottom (L.B.) section, Base (0) of the Bottom (Ground) Platform and Player II maintains the Red-Purple color band Black pieces that station at the Upper Bottom (U.B.) section, Base (0) also of the Bottom Platform. Chess Set # 1 uses the conventional, uniform position (both Player I and Player II Orange-Blue color band pieces' initial position configuration are at the Top Platform) for the VERTICAL method of movement for the pieces. Chess Set # 2 uses the non-conventional, uniform position (because both Player I and Player II Orange-Red pieces' initial position configuration are at the Top Platform) for the HORIZONTAL method of movement of the pieces. Chess Set # 3 uses the conventional, uniform position (because both Player I and Player II Red-Purple color band pieces' initial position configuration are at the Bottom (Ground) Platform) for the VERTICAL method of movement for the pieces.

Photo 25/ # 8223 –AIR-TO-GROUND/GROUND-TO-GROUND/AIR-TO-AIR(A-G)/(G-G)/(A-A) -illustrates a possible initial position configuration for a Triple Set Game. Chess Set # 1 is the Orange-Blue color band chess set represented by the first group of letters (A-G), Chess Set # 2 is the Orange-Red color band chess set represented by the second group of letters(G-G) and Chess Set # 3 is the Red-Purple color band set represented by the third group of letters (A-A). With regards to Chess Set # 1, Player I controls the Orange-Blue color band White pieces that position at the Lower Top (L.T.) section, Base (1) of the Top (Air) Platform and Player II maintains the Orange-Blue color band pieces that station at the Upper Bottom (U.B.) section, Base (0), of the Bottom (Ground) Platform. Concerning Chess Set # 2, Player I controls the Orange-Red color band Black pieces that position at the Bottom Left (B.L.) section, Base (0) of the Bottom (Ground) Platform and Player II maintains the Orange-Red color band White pieces that station at the Bottom Right(B.R.) section, Base (0), also of the Bottom Platform. In reference to Chess Set # 3, Player I controls the Red-Purple color band White pieces that position at the Top Right (T.R.) section, Base (1) of the Top (Air) Platform and Player II maintains the Red-Purple color band Black pieces that station at the Top Left (T.L.) section, Base (1) also of the Top Platform. Chess Set # 1 uses the conventional, non-uniform position (because Player I Orange-Blue color band White pieces are at the Top Platform and Player II Orange-Blue color band Black pieces' initial position configuration are at the Bottom Platform) for the VERTICAL method of movement of the pieces. Chess Set # 2 uses the non-conventional, uniform position (because both Player I and Player II Orange-Red color band pieces initial position configuration are at the Bottom Platform) which requires the HORIZONTAL method of movement of the pieces. Chess Set # 3 uses the conventional, uniform position (because both Player I and Player II Red-Purple color band pieces' initial position configuration are at the Top Platform) which requires the HORIZONTAL method of movement for the pieces.

Folder 23/ # 8905 – Discloses the initial set-up for the Quadruple Set Game (Q.4.1.1) having an initial positional configuration of GROUND-TO-GROUND/GROUND-TO-GROUND/AIR-TO-AIR/AIR-TO-AIR (G-G)/(G-G)/(A-A)/(A-A). Chess Set # 1 is the Orange-Blue color band set. Chess Set # 2 is the Orange-Red color band set. Chess Set # 3 is the Red-Purple color band set. Chess Set # 4 is the Red-Yellow color band set.

Regarding Chess Set # 1, Player I controls the Orange-Blue color band White pieces that position at the Lower Bottom (L.B.) section, Base (0) of the Bottom (Ground) Platform AND Player II maintains the Orange-Blue color band Black pieces that stations at the Upper Bottom (U.B.) section, Base (0) also of the Bottom (Ground) Platform. Thus, the nomenclature (G-G) for the first letter group is Chess Set # 1.

Concerning Chess Set # 2, the Orange-Red color band set, Player I controls the Orange-Red color band Black pieces that position at the Bottom Left (B.L.) section, Base (0) of the Bottom (Ground) Platform AND Player II maintains the Orange-Red color band White pieces that stations at the Bottom Right (B.R.) section, Base (0) also of the Bottom (Ground) Platform. Thus the nomenclature (G-G) for the second letter group is Chess Set # 2.

Regarding Chess Set # 3, the Red-Purple color band set, Player I controls the Red-Purple color band White pieces that position at the Lower Top (L.T.) section, Base (1) of the Top (Air) Platform AND Player II maintains the Red-Purple color band Black pieces that station at the Upper Top (U.T.) Platform, Base (1), also of the Top (Air) Platform. Thus the nomenclature (A-A) for the third letter group is Chess Set # 3.

Concerning Chess Set # 4, the Red-Yellow color band set, Player I controls the Red-Yellow color band Black pieces that position at the Top Left (T.L.) section of the Top (Air) Platform AND Player II maintains the Red-Yellow color band White pieces that station at the Top Right (T.R.) section, also of the Top (Air) Platform.

Folder 23/ # 8906 – Illustrates the initial set-up for the Quadruple Set game, (Q.4.1.2) having an initial positional configuration of GROUND-TO-AIR/GROUND-TO-GROUND/AIR-TO-GROUND/AIR-TO-AIR (G-A)/(G-G)/(A-G)/A-A). Chess Set # 1 is the Orange-Blue color band set. Chess Set # 2 is the Orange-Red color band set. Chess Set # 3 is the Red-Purple color band set. Chess Set # 4 is the Red-Yellow color band set.

Regarding Chess Set # 1,Player I controls the Orange-Blue color band White pieces that position at the Lower Bottom (L.B.) section, Base (0) of the Bottom (Ground) Platform AND Player II maintains the Orange-Blue color band Black pieces that station at the Upper Top (U.T.) section, Base (1) of the Top (Air) Platform.

Concerning Chess Set # 2,Player I controls the Orange-Red color band Black pieces that position at the Bottom Left (B.L.) section, Base (0) of the Bottom (Ground) Platform AND Player II maintains the Orange-Red color band White pieces that station at the Bottom Right (B.R.) section, Base (0) also of the Bottom (Ground) Platform.

Regarding Chess Set # 3,Player I controls the Red-Purple color band White pieces that position at the Lowe Top (L.T.) section, Base (1) of the Top (Air) Platform AND Player II maintains the Red-Purple color band Black pieces that station at the Upper Bottom (U.B.) section, Base (0) of the Bottom Platform.

Concerning Chess Set # 4, Player I controls the Red-Yellow color band Black pieces that position at the Top Left (T.L.) section, Base (1) of the Top (Air) Platform AND Player II maintains the Red-Yellow color band White pieces that station at the Top Right (T.R.) section, Base (1) of the Top (Air) Platform.

Folder 23 / # 8907 – Displays the initial set-up for the Quadruple Set Game (Q.4.1.3) having an initial positional configuration of GROUND-TO-AIR/AIR-TO-GROUND/AIR-TO-GROUND/GROUND-TO-AIR (G-A)/(A-G)/(A-G)/(G-A). Chess Set # 1 is the Orange-Blue color band set. Chess Set # 2 is the Orange-Red color band set. Chess Set # 3 is the Red-Purple color band set. Chess Set # 4 is the Red-Yellow color band set.

Regarding Chess Set # 1,Player I Orange-Blue color band White pieces position at the Lower Bottom (L.B.) section, Base (0) of the Bottom (Ground) Platform AND Player II Orange-Blue color band Black pieces station at the Upper Top (U.T.) section, Base (1) of the Top (Air) Platform.

Concerning Chess Set # 2,Player I Orange-Red color band Black pieces position at the Top Left (T.L.) section, Base (1) of the Top (Air) Platform AND Player II Red-Purple color band Black pieces station at the Bottom Right (B.R.) section, Base (0) of the Bottom (Ground) Platform.

Regarding Chess Set #3,Player I Red-Purple color band White pieces position at the Lower Top (L.T.) section, Base (1) of the Top (Air) Platform AND Player II Red-Purple color band Black pieces station at the Upper Bottom (U.B.) section, Base (0) of the Bottom (Ground) Platform.

Concerning Chess Set # 4,Player I Red-Yellow color band Black pieces position at the Bottom Left (B.L.) section, Base (0) of the Bottom (Ground) Platform AND Player II Red-Yellow color band White pieces station at the Top Right (T.R.) section, Base (1) of the Top (Air) Platform.

Folder 23 / # 8908 – Displays the initial set-up for the Quadruple Set Game (Q4.1.4) having an initial position configuration of AIR-TO-AIR/AIR-TO-GROUND/ GROUND-TO-GROUND/GROUND-TO-AIR (A-A)/(A-G)/(G-G)/(G-A). Chess Set # 1 is the Orange-Blue color band set. Chess Set # 2 is the Orange-Red color band set. Chess Set # 3 is the Red-Purple color band set. Chess Set # 4 is the Red-Yellow color band set.

Regarding Chess Set # 1, Player I controls the Orange-Blue color band White pieces that position at the Lower Top (L.T.) section, Base (1) of the Top (Air) Platform AND Player II maintains the Orange-Blue color band Black pieces that station at the Upper Top (U.T.) section, Base (1) of the Top (Air) Platform.

Concerning Chess Set # 2, Player I controls the Orange-Red color band Black pieces that position at the Top Left (T.L.) section, Base (1) of the Top (Air) Platform AND Player II maintains the Orange-Red color band White pieces that station at the Bottom Right (B.R.) section, Base (0) of the Bottom (Ground) Platform.

Regarding Chess Set # 3, Player I controls the Red-Purple color band White pieces that position at the Lower Bottom (L.B.) section, Base (0) of the Bottom (Ground) Platform AND Player II maintains the Red-Purple color band Black pieces that station at the Upper Bottom (U.B.) section, Base (0) of the Bottom (Ground) Platform.

Concerning Chess Set # 4, Player I Red-Yellow color band Black pieces position at the Bottom Left (B.L.) section, Base (0) of the Bottom (Ground) Platform AND Player II maintains the Red-Yellow color band White pieces that station at the Top Right (T.R.) section, Base (1) of the Top (Air) Platform.

Folder 23 / # 8909 – Illustrates the initial set-up for the Quadruple Set Game (Q.4.1.5) having an initial position configuration of AIR-TO-AIR/AIR-TO-AIR/GROUND-TO-GROUND/GROUND-TO-GROUND (A-A)/(A-A)/(G-G)/(G-G). Chess Set # 1 is the Orange-Blue color band set. Chess Set # 2 is the Orange-Red color band set. Chess Set # 3 is the Red-Purple color band set. Chess Set # 4 is the Red-Yellow color band set.

Regarding Chess Set # 1, Player I controls the Orange-Blue color band White pieces position at the Lower Top (L.T.) section, Base (1) of the Top (Air) Platform AND Player II maintains the Orange-Blue color band Black pieces station at the Upper Top (U.T.) section, Base (1), also at the Top (Air) Platform.

Concerning Chess Set # 2, Player I controls the Orange-Red color band Black pieces position at the Top Left (T.L.) section, Base (1) of the Top (Air) Platform AND Player II maintains the Orange-Red color band White pieces that station at the Top Right (T.R.) section, Base (1) of the Top (Air) Platform.

Regarding Chess Set #3, Player I controls the Red-Purple color band White pieces that position at the Lower Bottom (L.B.) section, Base (0), of the Bottom (Ground) Platform AND Player II maintains the Red-Purple color band Black pieces that station at the Upper Bottom (U.B.) section, Base (0), of the Bottom (Ground) Platform.

Concerning Chess Set # 4, Player I controls the Red-Yellow color band Black pieces that position at the Bottom Left (B.L.) section, Base (0) of the Bottom (Ground) Platform AND Player II maintains the Red-Yellow color band White pieces that station at the Bottom Right (B.R.) section, Base (0) of the Bottom (Ground) Platform.

EQUATIONS FOR THE QUADRUPLE SET GAME,(Q.4.1.1)-(G-G)/(G-G)/(A-A)/ (A-A)-BOOK 4 VOL. 1 GAME 1, MODEL III.

1. R.Y.   (I b(P (alpha prime) 2/ P (alpha prime) 7) - I b(P B2/ P B7) ;
           T.L.(1)   T.L.(1)   T.C.(1)   T.C.(1)
   ; II w(P (alpha prime) 1 / P (alpha prime) 8) - II w(P G1/ P G8)).
       T.R.(1)   T.R.(1)   B.C.(0)   B.C.(0)

In Equation 1,part 1,Sections(A/B),for Section(A),Player I (first) Red-Yellow color band Black Pawn that positions at Row(alpha prime),Column(2),Top Left(T.L.) section, Base (1),uses the Direct Physical two spaces <u>horizontal</u> (Chess Set # 4,the fourth group of letters, having an (A-A), initial positional configuration) movement to displace to Row(B),Column (2),Top Center(T.C.) Platform, Base(1) AND for Section(B),Player I (second) Black Pawn that positions at Row(alpha prime),Column(7),Top Left(T.L.) section, Base(1) also uses the two spaces movement to displace to Row(B),Column(7),Top Center(T.C.) Platform, Base (1).

In Equation 1,part 2,Sections(C/D),for Section(C),Player II (first) Red-Yellow color band White Pawn that stations at Row(alpha prime),Column(1),*Top Right(T.R.) section, Base (1),uses the *Direct Abstract two spaces <u>horizontal</u> movement to displace to Row(G), Column(1),*Bottom Center(B.C.) Platform, Base(0) AND for Section(D),Player II (second) Red-Yellow color band White Pawn that stations at Row(alpha prime),Column(8), *Top Right (T.R.) section, Base(1),also uses the* Direct Abstract two spaces movement (onto the immediate second available vacant squares) to displace to Row(G),Column(8), *Bottom Center(B.C.) Platform, Base(0).

2. R.P.   (I w(P (alpha) B / P (alpha) G) - I w(P 3B/ P 3G)   ;
           L.T.(1)   L.T.(1)   T.C.(1)   B.C.(0)
   ; II b(P (alpha) B / P (alpha) G) - II b(P 6B/ P 6G)).
       U.T.(1)   U.T.(1)   T.C.(1)   B.C.(0)

In Equation 2,part 1,Sections(A/B),for Section(A),Player I (first) Red-Purple color band White Pawn that positions at Row(alpha),Column(B),Lower Top(L.T.) section, Base(1),uses the Direct Physical two spaces <u>vertical</u> (Chess Set # 3,the third group of letters, having an (A-A) initial positional configuration) movement to displace (onto the immediate second available vacant square) to Row(3),Column(B),Top Center(T.C.) Platform, Base(1) AND for Section(B),Player II (second) Black Pawn that stations at Row(alpha),Column(G), *Lower Top(L.T.) section, Base(1),also uses the *Direct Abstract two spaces movement to displace to Row(3), Column(G),*Bottom Center(B.C.) Platform, Base(0).

In Equation 2,part 2,Sections(C/D),for Section(C),Player II (first) Red-Purple color band Black Pawn that stations at Row(alpha),Column(B),Upper Top(U.T.) section, Base(1),uses the Direct Physical two spaces <u>vertical</u> movement to displace (onto the immediate second available vacant square) to Row(6),Column(B) Top Center(T.C.) Platform, Base(1) AND for Section(D),Player II (second) Black Pawn that stations at Row(alpha),Column(G),*Upper Top(U.T.) section, Base(1),uses the *Direct Abstract two spaces movement to displace to Row(6),Column(G),*Bottom Center(B.C.) Platform, Base(0).

3. O.R.   (I b(P (alpha prime) 2 / P (alpha prime) 3) - I b(P C2/ P C3)   ;
          B.L.(0)   B.L.(0)   T.C.(1)   T.C.(1)
; II w(P (alpha prime) 1/ P (alpha prime) 8) - II w(P F1/ P F8)).
     B.R.(0)   B.R.(0)   B.C.(0)   B.C.(0)

In Equation 3,part 1,Sections(A/B),for Section(A),Player I (first) Orange-Red color band Black Pawn that positions at Row(alpha prime),Column(2),*Bottom Left (B.L.) section, Base (0),uses the *Direct Abstract two spaces <u>horizontal</u> (Chess Set # 2,the second group of letters, having a (G-G) initial positional configuration) movement to displace to Row(C),Column(2),*Top Center(T.C.) Platform, Base(1) AND for Section(B),Player I (second) Black Pawn that positions at Row(alpha prime), Column(3),*Bottom Left(B.L.) section, Base(0),also uses the *Direct Abstract two spaces movement to displace (onto the immediate second available vacant square) to Row(C), Column(3),*Top Center(T.C.) Platform, Base(1).

In Equation 3,part 2,Sections(C/D),for Section(C),Player II (first) Orange-Red color band White Pawn that stations at Row(alpha prime),Column(1,Bottom Right(B.R.) section, Base(0),uses the Direct Physical two spaces <u>horizontal</u> movement to displace (onto the second immediate available vacant square) to Row(F),Column (1),Bottom Center(B.C.) Platform, Base(0) AND for Section(D),Player II (second) White Pawn that stations at Row(alpha prime),Column(8),Bottom Right(B.R.) section, Base(0),also uses the Direct Physical two spaces movement to displace to Row(F),Column(8),Bottom Center(B.C.) Platform, Base(0).

4. O.B.   (I w(P (alpha) B / P (alpha) C) - I w(P 4B / P 4C) ;
            L.B.(0)   L.B.(0)   T.C.(1)   T.C.(1)
; II b(P (alpha) F / P (alpha) G) - II b(P 7F / P 7G)).
    U.B.(0)   U.B.(0)   T.C.(1)   T.C.(1)

In Equation 4,part 1,Sections(A/B),for Section(A),Player I (first) Orange-Blue color band White Pawn that positions at Row(alpha),Column(B),*Lower Bottom(L.B.) section, Base(0) uses the *Direct Abstract two spaces <u>vertical</u> (Chess Set # 1,the first group of letters, having a (G-G) initial positional configuration) movement (onto the second immediate available vacant squares) to displace to Row(4), Column(B),*Top Center(T.C.) Platform, Base(1) AND for Section(B),Player I (second) White Pawn that positions at Row(alpha), Column (C),*Lower Bottom (L.B.) section, Base(0) also uses the *Direct Abstract two spaces movement to displace to Row(4),Column(C),*Top Center(T.C.) Platform, Base(1).

In Equation 4,part 2,Sections(C/D),for Section(C),Player II (first) Orange-Blue color band Black Pawn that stations at Row(alpha),Column(F),*Upper Bottom(U.B.) section, Base(0), uses the *Direct Abstract two spaces <u>vertical</u> movement to displace to Row(7),Column(F), *Top Center(T.C.) Platform, Base(1) AND for Section(D), Player II (second) Black Pawn that stations at Row(alpha),Column(G), *Upper Bottom(U.B.) section, Base(0),also uses the *Direct Abstract two spaces movement to displace to Row(7),Column(G),*Top Center (T.C.) Platform, Base(1).

5. R.Y.   (I b(P (alpha prime) 3/ P (alpha prime) 4) - I b(P D3/ P D4)   ;
            T.L.(1)   T.L.(1)   T.C.(1)   T.C.(1)
; II w(P (alpha prime) 3/ P (alpha prime) 6) - II w(P F3/ P F6)   ).
    T.R.(1)   T.R.(1)   B.C.(0)   B.C.(0)

In Equation 5,part 1,Sections(A/B),for Section(A),Player I Red-Yellow color band Black Pawn that positions at Row(alpha prime),Column(3),Top Left(T.L.) section, Base(1) uses the Direct Physical two spaces <u>horizontal</u> (Chess Set # 4,the fourth group of letters, having an (A-A) initial positional configuration),movement to displace (onto the second immediate available vacant squares) to Row(D),Column (3),Top Center(T.C.) Platform, Base(1) AND for Section(B),Player I (second) Black Pawn that positions at Row(alpha prime),Column(4), Top Left(T.L.) section, Base (1),also uses the Direct Physical two spaces movement to displace to Row(D), Column(4),Top Center(T.C.) Platform, Base(1).

In Equation 5,part 2,Sections(C/D),for Section(C),Player II (first) Red-Yellow color band White Pawn that stations at Row(alpha prime),Column(3),*Top Right(T.R.) section, Base (1) uses the *Direct Abstract two spaces <u>horizontal</u> movement to displace to Row(F), Column(3),*Bottom Center(B.C.) Platform, Base(0) AND for Section(D),Player II (second) White Pawn that stations at Row(alpha prime),Column (6),*Top Right(T.R.) section, Base (1),also uses the *Direct Abstract two spaces movement to displace to Row(F),Column(6), *Bottom Center(B.C.) Platform, Base(0).

6. R.P.   (I w(P (alpha) A / P (alpha) C)   -   I w(P 2A / P 2C)   ;
               L.T.(1)   L.T.(1)   B.C.(0)   B.C.(0)
   ; II b(P (alpha) F / P (alpha) H)   -   II b(P 7F / P 7H)).
         U.T.(1)   U.T.(1)   B.C.(0)   T.C.(1)

In Equation 6,part 1,Sections(A/B),for Section(A),Player I (first) Red-Purple color band White Pawn that positions at Row(alpha),Column(A),*Lower Top(L.T.) section, Base(1) uses the *Direct Abstract two spaces <u>vertical</u> (Chess Set # 3,the third group of letters, having an (A-A) initial positional configuration) movement to displace(onto the second immediate available vacant squares) to Row(2),Column(A), *Bottom Center(B.C.) Platform, Base(0) AND for Section(B),Player I (second) White Pawn that positions at Row(alpha), Column(C),*Lower Top(L.T.) section, Base(1), also uses the *Direct Abstract two spaces movement to displace to Row(2),Column (C),Bottom Center(B.C.) Platform, Base(0).

In Equation 6,part 2,Sections(C/D),for Section(C),Player II (first) Red-Purple color band Black Pawn that stations at Row(alpha),Column(F),*Upper Top(U.T.) section, Base(1),uses the *Direct Abstract two spaces <u>vertical</u> movement to displace to Row (7),Column(F),* Bottom Center(B.C.) Platform, Base(0) AND for Section(D), Player II (second) Black Pawn that stations at Row(alpha),Column(H), Upper Top(U.T.) section, Base(1),uses the Direct Physical two spaces movement to displace to Row (7),Column(H) , Top Center(T.C.) Platform, Base(1).

7. O.R. (I b(P (alpha prime) 7/ P (alpha prime) 8)   -   I b(P B7 / P B8)   ;
               B.L.(0)   B.L.(0)   B.C.(0)   B.C.(0)
   ; II w(P (alpha prime) 3/ P (alpha prime) 7)   -   II w(P E3 / P E7)   ).
         B.R.(0)   B.R.(0)   B.C.(0)   T.C.(1)

In Equation 7,part 1,Section(A/B),for Section(A),Player I Orange-Red color band Black Pawn that positions at Row(alpha prime),Column(7),Bottom Left(B.L.) section, Base(0), uses the Direct Physical two spaces <u>horizontal</u> (Chess Set # 2,the second group of letters, having a (G-G) initial positional configuration) movement to displace to Row(B),Column (7),Bottom Center(B.C.) Platform, Base(0) AND for Section(B),Player I (second) Black Pawn that positions at Row(alpha prime),Column

(8),Bottom Left(B.L.) section, Base(0), also uses the Direct Physical two spaces movement to displace to Row(B),Column(8), Bottom Center(B.C.) Platform, Base(0).

In Equation 7,part 2,Sections(C/D),for Section(C),Player II (first) Orange-Red color band White Pawn that stations at Row(alpha prime),Column(3),Bottom Right(B.R.) section, Base (0),uses the Direct Physical two spaces <u>horizontal</u> movement to displace to Row(E), Column(3),Bottom Center(B.C.) Platform, Base(0) AND for Section(D),Player II (second) White Pawn that stations at Row(alpha prime), Column(7),*Bottom Right(B.R.) section, Base(0),uses the *Direct Abstract two spaces movement to displace to Row(E), Column(7),* Top Center(T.C.) Platform, Base(1).

8. O.B. (I w (P (alpha) F / P (alpha) G) - I w(P 4F / P 4G)   ;
           L.B.(0)   L.B.(0)   B.C.(0)   B.C.(0)
 ; II b(P (alpha) C / P (alpha) D) - II b(P 7C / P 7D)).
      U.B.(0)   U.B.(0)   B.C.(0)   B.C.(0)

In Equation 8,part 1,Sections(A/B),for Section(A),Player I (first) Orange-Blue color band White Pawn that positions at Row(alpha),Column(F),Lower Bottom(L.B.) section, Base(0) uses the Direct Physical two spaces <u>vertical</u> (Chess Set # 1,the first group of letters, having a (G-G) initial positional configuration) movement (onto the immediate second available vacant squares) to displace to Row(4),Column(F), Bottom Center(B.C.) Platform, Base(0) AND for Section(B),Player I (second) White Pawn that positions at Row(alpha),Column (G),Lower Bottom(L.B.) section, Base (0),also uses the Direct Physical two spaces movement to displace to Row(4),Column(G),Bottom Center(B.C.) Platform, Base(0).

In Equation 8,part 2,Sections(C/D),for Section(C),Player II (first) Orange-Blue color band Black Pawn that stations at Row(alpha),Column(C),Upper Bottom(U.B.) section, Base(0), uses the Direct Physical two spaces <u>vertical</u> movement to displace to Row(7),Column(C), Bottom Center(B.C.) Platform, Base(0) AND for Section(D), Player II (second) Black Pawn that stations at Row(alpha),Column(D),Upper Bottom(U.B.) section ,Base(0),also uses the Direct Physical two spaces movement to displace to Row(7),Column(D),Bottom Center (B.C.) Platform, Base(0).

9. R.Y. (I b(P (alpha prime) 5 / P (alpha prime) 6)   -   I b(P B5 / P B6) ;
          T.L.(1)   T.L.(1)   B.C.(0)   B.C.(0)
 ; II w(Kn (gamma prime) 3/ Kn (gamma prime) 6) - II w(Kn H4/ Kn H5)).
      T.R.(1)   T.R.(1)   T.C.(1)   T.C.(1)

In Equation 9,part 1,Sections(A/B),for Section(A),Player I (first) Red-Yellow color band Black Pawn that positions at Row(alpha prime),Column(5),*Top Left(T.L.) section, Base (1), uses the *Direct Abstract two spaces <u>horizontal</u> (Chess Set # 4,the fourth group of letters, having an (A-A) positional configuration) movement (onto the immediate second available vacant square) to displace to Row(B),Column (5), *Bottom Center(B.C.) Platform, Base(0) AND for Section(B),Player I (second) Black Pawn that positions at Row(alpha prime),Column(6),*Top Left(T.L.) section, Base (1),also uses the *Direct Abstract two spaces movement to displace to Row(B), Column (6),*Bottom Center(B.C.) Platform, Base(0).

In Equation 9,part 2,Sections(C/D),for Section(C),Player II (first) Red-Yellow color band White Knight that stations at Row(gamma prime),Column(3),Top Right(T.R.) section, Base (1),uses the Direct Physical 4/2 squares movement to displace to Row (H),Column(4), Top Center(T.C.) Platform, Base(1) AND for Section(D),Player II (second) White Knight that stations at Row(gamma prime),Column(6),Top Right (T.R.) section, Base(1),also uses the Direct Physical 4/2 squares movement to displace to Row(H),Column(5),Top Center(T.C.) Platform, Base(1).

10. R.P. (I w(P (alpha) F / P (alpha) H) - I w(P 2F/ P 2H) ;
            L.T.(1)   L.T.(1)   T.C.(1)   T.C.(1)
 ; II b(P (alpha) C / P (alpha) D) - II b(P 6C/ P 6D)).
 U.T.(1)   U.T.(1)   B.C.(0)   B.C.(0)

In Equation 10,part 1,Sections(A/B),Player I Red-Purple color band White Pawn that positions at Row(alpha),Column(F),Lower Top(L.T.) section, Base(1),uses the Direct Physical two spaces vertical (Chess Set # 3,the third group of letters, having an (A-A) initial positional configuration) movement (onto the second immediate available vacant square) to displace to Row(2),Column(F),Top Center(T.C.) Platform, Base(1) AND for Section(B), Player I (second) White Pawn that positions at Row(alpha),Column(H),Lower Top(L.T.) section, Base(1),uses the Direct Physical two spaces movement to displace to Row(2), Column(H), Top Center(T.C.) Platform, Base(1).

In Equation 10,part 2,Sections(C/D),for Section(C),Player II Red-Purple color band Black Pawn that stations at Row(alpha),Column(C),*Upper Top(U.T.) section, Base(1),uses the *Direct Abstract two spaces vertical movement to displace (onto the second immediate available vacant square) to Row(6),Column(C),*Bottom Center (B.C.) Platform, Base(0) AND for Section(D),Player II (second) Black Pawn that stations at Row(alpha),Column (D),*Upper Top(U.T.) section, Base(1),also uses the *Direct Abstract two spaces movement to displace to Row(6),Column(D), *Bottom Center(B.C.) Platform, Base(0).

11. O.R. (I b(P (alpha prime) 4/ P (alpha prime) 5) - I b(P B4 / P C5) ;
            B.L.(0)   B.L.(0)   B.C.(0)   B.C.(0)
 ; II w(P (alpha prime) 2 / P (alpha prime) 6) - II w (P E2 / P E6)).
  B.R.(0)   B.R.(0)   T.C.(1)   B.C.(0)

In Equation 11,part 1,Sections(A/B),for Section(A),Player I (first) Orange-Red color band Black Pawn that positions at Row(alpha prime),Column(4),Bottom Left(B.L.) section, Base(0),uses the Direct Physical two spaces horizontal (Chess Set # 2,the second group of letters, having a (G-G) initial positional configuration) movement (onto the second immediate available vacant square) to displace to Row(B),Column (4),Bottom Center(B.C.) Platform, Base(0) AND for Section(B),Player II (second) Black Pawn that positions at Row(alpha prime),Column(5),Bottom Left(B.L.) section, Base(0),also uses the Direct Physical two spaces movement to displace to Row(C), Column(5),Bottom Center(B.C.) Platform, Base(0).

In Equation 11,part 2,Sections(C/D),for Section(C),Player II Orange-Red color band White Pawn that stations at Row(alpha prime),Column(2),*Bottom Right(B.R.) section, Base(0), uses the *Direct Abstract two spaces horizontal movement to displace to Row(E),Column (2),*Top Center(T.C.) Platform, Base(1) AND for Section(D),Player II (second) White Pawn that stations at Row(alpha prime), Column(6),Bottom Right(B.R.) section, Base(0),uses the Direct Physical two spaces movement to displace to Row(E), Column(6),Bottom Center (B.C.) Platform, Base(0).

12. O.B. (I w(B(gamma) D/ B (gamma) E) - I w(B (alpha) B/ B (alpha) G) ;
       L.B.(0)   L.B.(0)   L.T.(1)   L.T.(1)
; II b(B (gamma) D / B (gamma) E) - II b(B (beta) E / B (beta) D)).
    U.B.(0)   U.B.(0)   U.B.(0)   U.B.(0)

In Equation 12,part 1,Sections(A/B),for Section(A),Player I (first) Orange-Blue color band White Bishop that positions at Row(gamma),Column(D),*Lower Bottom(L.B.) section, Base(0),uses the *Direct Abstract diagonal movement to displace to Row (alpha),Column (B),*Lower Top(L.T.) section, Base(1) AND for Section(B),Player I (second) White Bishop that positions at Row(gamma),Column(E),*Lower Bottom (L.B.) section, Base(0),also uses the *Direct Abstract diagonal movement to displace to Row(alpha),Column(G),*Lower Top (L.T.) section, Base(1).

In Equation 12,part 2,Sections(C/D),for Section(C),Player II (first) Orange-Blue color band Black Bishop that stations at Row(gamma),Column(D),Upper Bottom (U.B.) section, Base (0),uses the Direct Physical diagonal movement to displace to Row(beta),Column(E),Upper Bottom(U.B.) section, Base(0) AND for Section(D), Player II (second) Black Bishop that stations at Row(gamma),Column(E),Upper Bottom(U.B.) section, Base(0),also uses the Direct Physical diagonal movement to displace to Row(beta),Column(D),Upper Bottom (U.B.) section, Base(0).

13. R.Y. (I b(B (gamma prime) 4 / B (gamma prime) 5) -
       T.L.(1)   T.L.(1)
 - I b(B (beta) D/B (beta) C) ;
       U.T.(1)   U.T.(1)
; II w(P G1 / P G8) - II w(P D1 / P D8)).
  B.C.(0)   B.C.(0)   B.C.(0)   B.C.(0)

In Equation 13,part 1,Sections(A/B),for Section(A),Player I (first) Red-Yellow color band Black Bishop that positions at Row(gamma prime),Column(4),Top Left(T.L.) section, Base(1),uses the Direct Physical diagonal movement to displace to Row (beta),Column(D), Upper Top(U.T.) section, Base(1) AND for Section(B),Player I (second) Black Bishop that positions at Row(gamma prime),Column(5),Top Left (T.L.) section, Base(1),also uses the Direct Physical diagonal movement to displace to Row(beta),Column(C),Upper Top(U.T.) section, Base(1).

In Equation 13,part 2,Sections(C/D),for Section(C),Player II (first) Red-Yellow color band White Pawn that stations at Row(G),Column(1),Bottom Center(B.C.) Platform, Base(0),uses the Direct Physical two spaces <u>horizontal</u> (Chess Set # 4,the Fourth Group having an (A-A) initial position set-up) movement (unto the second immediate available vacant square) to displace to Row(D),Column(1),Bottom Center (B.C.) Platform, Base(0) AND for Section(D),Player II (second) White Pawn that stations at Row(G),Column(8),Bottom Center(B.C.) Platform, Base(0),also uses the two spaces movement (unto the second immediate available vacant square) to displace to Row(D),Column(8),Bottom Center(B.C.) Platform, Base(0).

14. R.P. (I w(B (gamma) D / B (gamma) E) - I w(B (beta) E / B (beta) D) ;
        L.T.(1)   L.T.(1)   L.B.(0)   L.B.(0)
; II b(C (beta) B / C (beta) G)   - II b (C 8B / C 8G)).
  U.T.(1)   U.T.(1)   T.C.(1)   T.C.(1)

In Equation 14,part 1,Sections(A/B),for Section(A),Player I (first) Red-Purple color band White Bishop that positions at Row(gamma),Column(D),*Lower Top(L.T.) section, Base (1), uses the *Direct Abstract diagonal movement to displace to Row (beta), Column (E), *Lower Bottom(L.B.) section, Base(0) AND for Section(B), Player I (second) White Bishop that positions at Row(gamma),Column(E),*Lower Top(L.T.) section, Base(1),also uses the *Direct Abstract diagonal movement to displace to Row(beta),Column(D),*Lower Bottom (L.B.) section, Base(0).

In Equation 14,part 2,Sections(C/D),for Section(C),Player II (first) Red-Purple color band Black Castle that stations at Row(beta),Column(B),Upper Top(U.T.) section, Base(1),uses the Direct Physical movement to displace to Row(8),Column(B),Top Center(T.C.) Platform, Base(1) AND for Section(D),Player II (second) Black Castle that stations at Row(beta), Column(G),Upper Top(U.T.) section, Base(1),uses the Direct Physical movement to displace to Row(8),Column(G),Top Center(T.C.) Platform, Base(1).

15. O.R. (I b(Kn (gamma prime) 3/ Kn (gamma prime)6)   -
          B.L.(0)   B.L.(0)
     - I b(Kn A2/ Kn A7) ;
     T.C.(1)   T.C.(1)
; II w(Kn (gamma prime) 3/ Kn (gamma prime) 6) - II w(Kn H4 / Kn H5)   ).
     B.R.(0)   B.R.(0)   B.C.(0)   B.C.(0)

In Equation 15,part 1,Sections(A/B),for Section(A),Player I (first) Orange-Red color band Black Knight that positions at Row(gamma prime),Column(3),*Bottom Left (B.L.) section, Base(0),uses the *Direct Abstract 4/2 squares movement to displace to Row(A),Column(2), *Top Center(T.C.) Platform, Base(1) AND for Section(B), Player I (second) Black Knight that positions at Row(gamma prime),Column(6), *Bottom Left(B.L.) section, Base(0),also uses the *Direct Abstract 4/2 squares movement to displace to Row(A),Column(7),*Top Center (T.C.) Platform, Base(1).

In Equation 15,part 2,Sections(C/D),for Section(C),Player II (first) Orange-Red color band White Knight that stations at Row(gamma prime),Column(3),Bottom Right(B.R.) section, Base(0),uses the Direct Physical 4/2 squares movement to displace to Row(H),Column(4), Bottom Center(B.C.) Platform, Base(0) AND for Section(D),Player II (second) White Bishop that stations at Row(gamma prime), Column(6),Bottom Right(B.R.) section, Base (0),uses the Direct Physical 4/2 squares movement to displace to Row(H),Column(5), Bottom Center(B.C.) Platform, Base(0).

16. O.B. (I w(Kn (gamma) C / Kn (gamma) F) - I w(Kn B1/ Kn G1) ;
          L.B.(0)   L.B.(0)   T.C.(1)   T.C.(1)
   ; II b(Kn (gamma) C / Kn (gamma) F) - II b(Kn 8D / Kn 8E)).
     U.B.(0)   U.B.(0)   T.C.(1)   T.C.(1)

In Equation 16,part 1,Sections(A/B),for Section(A),Player I (first) Orange-Blue color band White Knight that positions at Row(gamma),Column(C),*Lower Bottom(L.B.) section, Base(0),uses the *Direct Abstract 4/2 squares movement to displace to Row (B), Column(1), *Top Center(T.C.) Platform, Base(1) AND for Section(B),Player I (second) White Knight that positions at Row(gamma), Column(F),*Lower Bottom (L.B.) section, Base(0),also uses the *Direct Abstract 4/2 squares movement to displace to Row(G),Column(1),*Top Center (T.C.) Platform, Base(1).

In Equation 16,part 2,Sections(C/D),for Section(C),Player II (first) Orange-Blue color band Black Knight that stations at Row(gamma),Column(C),*Upper Bottom (U.B.) section, Base (0),uses the *Direct Abstract 4/2 squares movement to displace to Row(8),Column(D), *Top Center(T.C.) Platform, Base(1) AND for Section(D), Player II (second) Black Knight that stations at Row(gamma), Column(F),*Upper Bottom(U.B.) section, Base(0),also uses the *Direct Abstract 4/2 squares movement to displace to Row(8),Column(E),*Top Center (T.C.) Platform, Base(1).

17A. R.Y. (I b(B (beta)C/Q (sigma prime) 5) -
          U.T.(1)   T.L.(1)
   - I b(B (alpha) D)/Q (gamma prime) 5) ;
         U.T.(1)   T.L.(1)
; II w(Kn H4 / Kn H5) - II w(Kn F5 / Kn F4)).
 T.C.(1)   T.C.(1)   T.C.(1)   T.C.(1)

In Equation 17,part 1,Sections(A/B),for Section(A),Player I Red-Yellow color band Black Bishop that positions at Row(beta),Column(C),Upper Top(U.T.) section, Base (1),uses the Direct Physical diagonal single space movement to displace to Row (alpha),Column(D), Upper Top(U.T.) section, Base(1) AND for Section(B), Player I Black Queen that stations at Row(sigma prime),Column(5),Top Left(T.L.) section, Base(1),uses the Direct Physical single space movement to displace to Row(beta), Column(C),Upper Top(U.T.) section, Base(1).

In Equation 17,part 2,Sections(C/D),for Section(C),Player II (first) Red-Yellow color band White Knight that stations at Row(H),Column(4),Top Center(T.C.) Platform, Base(1),uses the Direct Physical 3/2 squares movement to displace to Row(F), Column(5),Top Center (T.C.) Platform, Base(1) AND for Section(D),Player II (second) Knight that stations at Row(H), Column(5),Top Center(T.C.) Platform, Base(1),also uses the Direct Physical 3/2 squares movement to displace to Row(F), Column(4),Top Center(T.C.) Platform, Base(1).

17B. R.Y. (I b(Q (gamma prime) 5 – Q (beta) C ; II w(Forfeits the turn to play)).
          T.L.(1)   U.T.(1)
18A. O.B. (I w(Ki (sigma) E/Q (sigma) D) - I w(Ki (gamma) D/Q (gamma) E) ;
        L.B.(0)   L.B.(0)   L.T.(1)   L.T.(1)
; II b(Ki (sigma) E / Q (sigma) D) - II b(Ki (gamma) D / Q (sigma) E)).
  U.B.(0)   U.B.(0)   U.B.(0)   U.B.(0)

In Equation 18A,part 1,Sections(A/B),for Section(A),Player I Orange-Blue color band White King that positions at Row(sigma),Column(E),*Lower Bottom(L.B.) section, Base(0),uses the *Direct Abstract single space movement to displace to Row(gamma),Column(D), *Lower Top(L.T.) section, Base(1) AND for Section(B), Player I White Queen that positions at Row(sigma),Column(E),*Lower Bottom (L.B.) section, Base(0),also uses the *Direct Abstract single space movement to displace to Row(gamma),Column(E),*Lower Top(L.T.) section, Base(1).

In Equation 18A,part 2,Sections(C/D),for Section(C),Player II Orange-Blue color band Black King that stations at Row(sigma),Column(E),Upper Bottom(U.B.) section, Base(0), uses the Direct Physical single space diagonal movement to displace to Row(gamma), Column(D),Upper Bottom (U.B.) section, Base(0) AND for Section(D),Player II Black Queen that stations at Row(sigma), Column (D), Upper

Bottom (U.B.) section, Base(0),also uses the Direct Physical single space movement to displace to Row(sigma),Column(E), Upper Bottom(U.B.) section, Base(0).

18B. O.B.(I w(Forfeits the turn to play) ;

   ;   II b(Ki (gamma) D/ Q (sigma) E - Ki (gamma) C / Q (gamma) F   )).
              U.B.(0)   U.B.(0)   U.B.(0)   U.B.(0)

19. O.R. (I b(Kn A2 / Kn A7) - I b(Kn (alpha) B / Kn (alpha) B)   ;
           T.C.(1)   T.C.(1)   L.B.(0)   U.T.(1)
; II w(B (gamma prime) 4/B (gamma prime) 5) -
    B.R.(0)   B.R.(0)
   - II w(B (gamma) D/B (sigma) D)   ).
        U.B.(0)   U.B.(0)

In Equation 19,part 1,Sections(A/B),for Section(A),Player I (first) Orange-Red color band Black Knight that positions at Row(A),Column(2),*Top Center(T.C.) Platform, Base(1) uses the * Direct Abstract 3/2 squares movement to displace to Row(alpha), Column(B),* Lower Bottom(L.B.) section, Base(0) AND for Section(B),Player I (second) Black Knight that positions at Row(A),Column(7),Top Center(T.C.) Platform, Base(1) uses the Direct Physical 3/2 squares movement to displace to Row(alpha), Column(B),Upper Top(U.T.) section, Base(1).

In Equation 19,part 2,Sections(C/D),for Section(C),Player II (first) Orange-Red color band White Bishop that station at Row(gamma prime),Column(4),Bottom Right(B.R.) section, Base(0),uses the Direct Physical diagonal movements to displace to Row(gamma),Column (D),Upper Bottom(U.B.) section, Base(0) AND for Section(D),Player II (second) White Bishop that stations at Row(gamma prime),Column(5),Bottom Right(B.R.) section, Base (0),uses the Direct Physical diagonal movement to displace to Row(sigma),Column(D), Upper Bottom(U.B.) section, Base(0).

20A. R.P. (I w(Ki (sigma) E/ Q (sigma) D) -
        L.T.(1)   L.T.(1)
  - I w(Ki (gamma) D/ Q (gamma) E)   ;
        L.B.(0)   L.B.(0)
; II b(Player II forfeits the turn to play)).

20B. R.Y. (I b(Ki (sigma prime) 4 – Ki (gamma prime) 4 ;
             T.L.(1)   T.L.(1)
 ; II w(Player II forfeits the turn to play)).

20C. R.P. (I w(Player I forfeits the turn to play)   ;
 ; II b(B (gamma) D/ B (gamma) E) -
    U.T.(1)   U.T.(1)
  - II b(B (sigma prime) 4/B (gamma prime) 5)).
     T.L.(1)   B.R.(0)

21A. R.P. (I w(B (beta) E/B (beta) D) -
            L.B.(0)   L.B.(0)
  - I w(B (beta) E) X II b(B (gamma prime) 5) /
     L.B.(0)   B.R.(0)
    / I w(B (beta) D – B (alpha) C) ;
     L.B.(0)   L.B.(0)
  ; II b(B (sigma prime) 4) X I w(C (beta) B)).
    T.L.(1)   L.T.(1)

In Equation 21,part 1,Section(A),Player I Red-Purple color band White Bishop that positions at Row(beta),Column(E),Lower Bottom(L.B.) section, Base(0),uses the Direct Physical diagonal attack movement to capture Player II Black Bishop that stations at Row (gamma prime),Column(5),Bottom Right(B.R.) section, Base(0) AND for Section(B), Player I (second) Bishop, that positions at Row(beta),Column (D),Lower Bottom(L.B.) section, Base(0),uses the Direct Physical single space movement to displace to Row(alpha) , Column(C),Lower Bottom(L.B.) section, Base(0).

In Equation 21,part 2,Section(C),Player II Red-Purple color band Black Bishop that stations at Row(sigma prime),Column(4),Top Left(T.L.) section, Base(1),uses the Direct Physical diagonal attack movement to capture Player I White Castle that positions at Row(beta), Column(B),Lower Top(L.T.) section, Base(1).

21B. R.P. (I w(P (alpha) E / Q (gamma) E) - I w(P 1E / Q (alpha) E) ;
              L.T.(1)   L.B.(0)   T.C.(1)   T.C.(1)
  ; II b(Kn (gamma) F - Kn (alpha) G)).
    U.T.(1)   U.T.(1)

In Equation 21B,part 1,Sections(A/B),for Section(A),Player I Red-Purple color band White Pawn that positions at Row(alpha),Column(E),Lower Top(L.T.) section, Base (1),uses the Direct Physical single space <u>vertical</u> (Chess Set # 3,the third Group, having an (A-A) initial position set-up) movement to displace to Row(1),Column (E), Top Center(T.C.) Platform, Base(1) AND for Section(B),Player I White Queen that positions at Row(gamma), Column (E),Lower Bottom(L.B.) section, Base(0),uses the Direct Abstract two spaces movement to displace to Row(alpha),Column(E),Top Center(T.C.) Platform, Base(1).

In Equation 21B,part 2,Section(C),Player II Red-Purple color band Black Knight that stations at Row(gamma),Column(F),Upper Top(U.T.) section, Base(1),uses the Direct Physical 3/2 squares movement to displace to Row(alpha),Column(G),Upper Top(U.T.) section, Base(1).

21C. R.P. (I w(Q (alpha) E - Q (gamma prime) 6) ; II b(Forfeits turn to play)).
             L.T.(1)   B.R.(0)

22. R.P. (I w(Q (gamma prime) 6) X II b(Ki (sigma) E) ; ....
         B.R.(0)   U.T.(1)   [END] 1.

In Equation 22,part 1,Player I Red-Purple color band White Bishop that positions at Row(gamma prime),Column(5),*Bottom Right(B.R.) section, Base(0),uses the *Direct Abstract diagonal Stealth (silent) [CHECKMATE] attack movement to capture Player II Black King that positions at Row(sigma),Column(D),*Upper Top(U.T.) section, Base(1).

Player I wins the Red-Purple color band set. [END] 1. The match continues with the Orange-Blue, Orange-Red and Red-Yellow color band sets.

23. R.Y. (I b(Kn (gamma prime) 3/ Kn (gamma prime) 6) -
             T.L.(1)   T.L.(1)
   - I b(Kn A4/ Kn A5) ;
      B.C.(0)   B.C.(0)
  ; II w(Kn F4/ Kn F5) X I b(P D3/ P D4)).
   T.C.(1)   T.C.(1)   T.C.(1)   T.C.(1)

In Equation 23,part 1,Sections(A/B),for Section(A),Player I (first) Red-Yellow color band Black Knight that positions at Row(gamma prime),Column(3),*Top Left(T.L.) section, Base(1), uses the *Direct Abstract 4/2 squares movement to displace to Row (A),Column(4), *Bottom Center(B.C.) Platform, Base(0) AND for Section(B),Player I (second) Black Knight that positions at Row(gamma prime),Column(6),*Top Left (T.L.) section, Base(1), also uses the *Direct Abstract 4/2 squares movement to displace to Row(A),Column(5), *Bottom Center(B.C.) Platform, Base(0).

In Equation 23,part 2,Sections(C/D),for Section(C),Player II (first) Red-Yellow color band White Knight that stations at Row(F),Column(4),Top Center(T.C.) Platform, Base(1),uses the Direct Physical 3/2 squares attack movement to capture Player I Black Pawn that positions at Row(D),Column(3),Top Center(T.C.) Platform, Base(1) AND for Section(D), Player II (second) White Knight that stations at Row(F), Column(5),Top Center(T.C.) Platform, Base(1), also uses the Direct Physical 3/2 squares movement to displace to Row (D),Column(4),Top Center(T.C.) Platform, Base(1).

24. O.R. (I b(C (beta prime) 2/ P (alpha prime) 1) - I b(C B2/ P B1) ;
          B.L.(0)   B.L.(0)   B.C.(0)   B.C.(0)
  ; II w(Kn H4 / Kn H5) - II w(Kn E5/ Kn E4)).
  B.C.(0)   B.C.(0)   B.C.(0)   B.C.(0)

In Equation 24,part 1,Sections(A/B),for Section(A),Player I Orange-Red color band Black Castle that positions at Row(beta prime),Column(2),Bottom Left(B.L.) section, Base(0), uses the Direct Physical movement to displace to Row(B), Column (2),Bottom Center(B.C.) Platform, Base(0) AND for Section(B),Player I Black Pawn that positions at Row(alpha prime),Column(1),Bottom Left(B.L.) section, Base(0), uses the Direct Physical two spaces <u>horizontal</u> (Chess Set # 2,the Second Group, having a (G-G) initial position set-up) movement to displace to Row(B),Column(1), Bottom Center(B.C.) Platform, Base(0).

In Equation 24,part 2,Sections(C/D),for Section(C),Player II (first) Orange-Red color band White Knight that stations at Row(H),Column(4),Bottom Center(B.C.) Platform, Base(0), uses the Direct Physical 4/2 squares movement to displace to Row(E),Column(5),Bottom Center(B.C.) Platform, Base(0) AND for Section(D), Player II (second) White Knight that stations at Row(H),Column(5),Bottom Center (B.C.) Platform, Base(0),also uses the Direct Physical 4/2 squares movement to displace to Row(E),Column(4),Bottom Center(B.C.) Platform, Base(0).

25A. O.R. (I b(B (gamma prime) 5 X   II w(B (gamma) D /
                    B.L.(0)   L.B.(0)
/   (I b(Kn (alpha) B – Kn C3) ;
     L.B.(0)   B.C.(0)
;   IIw(Kn E4) X I b(Kn C3) / II w(Kn E5 – Kn C6)).
     B.C.(0)   B.C.(0)   B.C.(0)   B.C.(0)

In Equation 25A,part 1,Sections(A/B),for Section(A),Player I Orange-Red color band   Black Bishop that positions at Row(gamma prime),Column(5),Bottom Left(B.L.) section, Base(0), uses the Direct Physical diagonal attack movement to capture Player II White Bishop that stations at Row(gamma),Column(D),Lower Bottom (L.B.) section, Base(0) AND for Section (B),Player I Black Knight that positions at Row(alpha),Column(B),Lower Bottom(L.B.) section, Base(0),uses the 4/2 squares movement to displace to Row(C),Column(3),Bottom Center(B.C.) Platform, Base(0).

In Equation 25A,part 2,Sections(C/D),for Section(C),Player II Orange-Red color band White Knight that stations at Row(E),Column(4),Bottom Center(B.C.) Platform, Base(0), uses the Direct Physical 3/2 squares attack movement to capture Player I Black Knight that positions at Row(C),Column(3),Bottom Center(B.C.) Platform, Base(0) AND for Section (D),Player II White Knight that stations at Row (E),Column(5),Bottom Center(B.C.) Platform, Base(0),uses the Direct Physical 3/2 squares movement to displace to Row(C), Column(6),Bottom Center(B.C.) Platform, Base(0).

LOGIC: In Equation 25A,part 2,Section(D),Player II White Knight that moves to Row(C), Column(6),Bottom Center(B.C.) Platform, Base(0),now poises an imminent Direct Abstract 4/2 squares THREAT to Player I Black Knight that positions at Row (alpha),Column(B), Upper Top(U.T.) section, Base(1).

25B. O.R. (I b(B (gamma) D/ B (gamma prime) 4)   -
                      U.B.(0)   B.L.(0)
  - I b(B (sigma) E / B (sigma) E) ;
       U.T.(1)   L.T.(1)
; II w(P F8 / P F1) - II w(P C8 / P   C1)   ).
   B.C.(0)   B.C.(0)   T.C.(1)   T.C.(1)

In Equation 25B,part 1,Sections(A/B),for Section(A),Player I (first) Orange-Red color band Black Bishop that positions at Row(gamma),Column(D),*Upper Bottom(U.B.) section, Base (0),uses the *Direct Abstract single space diagonal movement to displace to Row (sigma),Column(E),*Upper Top(U.T.) section, Base (1) AND for Section(B),Player I (second) Black Bishop that positions at Row (gamma prime),Column(4),*Bottom Left(B.L.) section, Base(0), also uses the *Direct Abstract diagonal movement to displace to Row (sigma),Column(E),*Lower Top (L.T.) section, Base(1).

In Equation 25B,part 2,Sections(C/D),for Section(C),Player II (first) White Pawn that stations at Row(F),Column(8),*Bottom Center(B.C.) Platform, Base(0),uses the *Direct Abstract two spaces horizontal (Chess Set # 2,the Second Group having a (G-G) initial position set-up) movement (unto the immediate second available vacant square) to displace to Row(C), Column(8),*Top Center(T.C.) Platform, Base(1) AND for Section(D),Player II (second) White Pawn that stations at Row(F),Column

(1),*Bottom Center(B.C.) Platform, Base(0), also uses the *Direct Abstract two movement to displace to Row(C),Column(1), *Top Center(T.C.) Platform, Base(1).

LOGIC: In Equation 25B,part 2,Section(C),Player II (first) White Pawn that stations at Row(C),Column(8),Top Center(T.C.) Platform, Base(1),now poises an imminent Direct Abstract single space diagonal THREAT to Player I Black Knight that positions at Row (alpha),Column(B), Upper Top(U.T.) section, Base(1).

LOGIC: In Equation 25B,part 2,Section(D),Player II (second) White Pawn that stations at Row(C),Column(1),Top Center(T.C.) Platform, Base(1),now poises an imminent Direct Abstract single space diagonal THREAT to Player I Black Castle that positions at Row(B), Column(2),Bottom Center(B.C.) Platform, Base(0).

25C. O.R. (I b(P C2 – P D2)/ I b(B (sigma) E)   X   II w(C (beta prime) 7) ;
          T.C.(1)   T.C.(1)   U.T.(1)   B.R.(0)
; II w(P C 1 / C (beta prime) 2)   X   I b(C B 2 / B (beta prime) 7)   ).
  T.C.(1)   B.R.(0)   B.C.(0)   B.R.(0)

In Equation 25C,part 1,Sections(A/B),for Section(A),Player I Orange-Red color band Black Pawn that positions at Row(C),Column(2),Top Center(T.C.) Platform, Base (1),uses the Direct Physical single space horizontal (Chess Set # 2,the Second Group having a (G-G) initial position set-up) movement to displace to Row(D),Column (2), Top Center(T.C.) Platform, Base(1) AND for Section(B),Player I Black Bishop that positions at Row(sigma), Column(E),*Upper Top(U.T.) section, Base(1),uses the *Direct Abstract diagonal attack movement to capture Player II White Castle that stations at Row(beta prime),Column(7), *Bottom Right(B.R.) section, Base(0).

In Equation 25C,part 2,Sections(C/D),for Section(C),Player II White Pawn that stations at Row(C),Column(1),*Top Center(T.C.) Platform, Base(1),uses the *Direct Abstract single space diagonal attack movement to capture Player I Black Castle that positions at Row(B), Column(2),*Bottom Center(B.C.) Platform, Base(0) AND for Section(B),Player II Black Castle that stations at Row(beta prime),Column(2), Bottom Right(B.R.) section, Base(0), uses the Direct Physical attack movement to capture Player I Black Bishop that positions at Row(beta prime),Column(7),Bottom Right(B.R.) section, Base(0).

26. O.R. (I b(B (sigma) E)   X   II w (Ki (sigma prime) 4) ; ....
        L.T.(1)   B.R.(0)   [END] 2.

In Equation 26,part 1,Player I Orange-Red color band Black Bishop that positions at Row(sigma),Column(E),*Lower Top(L.T.) section, Base(1),uses the *Direct Abstract diagonal Stealth (silent) [CHECKMATE] attack movement to capture Player II White King that stations at Row(sigma prime),Column(4),*Bottom Right(B.R.) section, Base(0).

LOGIC: In Equation 25C,Section(D),the movement of Player II White Castle that stations at Row(beta prime),Column(2),Bottom Right(B.R.) section, Base(0) to capture Player I Black Bishop that positions at Row(beta prime),Column(7),Bottom Right(B.R.) section, Base(0),leaves an opening for Player I Black Bishop that positions at Row(sigma),Column (E),Lower Top(L.T.) section, Base(1) to launch a successful Direct Abstract Stealth(silent) diagonal [CHECKMATE] attack to capture Player II White

King that stations at Row (sigma prime),Column(4),Bottom Right(B.R.) section, Base(0). Player II White Queen should have been used to capture Player I Black Bishop at Row(beta prime),Column (7), Bottom Right(B.R.) section, Base(0).

Player I wins the Orange-Red color band set. [END] 2. The match continues with the Red-Yellow and Orange-Blue color band sets.

27A. R.Y. (I b(B (alpha) D/ Q (beta) C) - I b(B (gamma) F/ Q (sigma) E) ;
            U.T.(1)   U.T.(1)   U.T.(1)   U.B.(0)
 ; II w(Kn D3/ Kn D4) X I b(Kn A4/ Kn A5)).
   T.C.(1)   T.C.(1)   B.C.(0)   B.C.(0)

In Equation 27,part 1,Sections(A/B),Player I Red-Yellow color band Black Bishop that positions at Row(beta),Column(C),Upper Top(U.T.) section, Base(1),uses the Direct Physical single space diagonal movement to displace to Row(gamma), Column(F),Upper Top(U.T.) section, Base(1) AND Player I Black Queen that positions at Row(beta),Column (C),*Upper Top(U.T.) section, Base(1),uses the *Direct Abstract diagonal movement to displace to Row(sigma),Column(E),*Upper Bottom(U.B.) section, Base(0).

In Equation 27,part 2,Sections(C/D),for Section(C),Player II (first) Red-Yellow color band White Knight that stations at Row(D),Column(3),*Top Center(T.C.) Platform, Base(1),uses the *Direct Abstract 4/2 squares attack movement to capture Player I (first) Black Knight that positions at Row(A),Column(4),*Bottom Center(B.C.) Platform, Base(0) AND for Section(D),Player II (second) White Knight that stations at Row(D),Column(4),Top Center (T.C.) Platform, Base(1),also uses the Direct Abstract 4/2 squares attack movement to capture Player I (second) Black Knight that positions at Row(A),Column(5),Bottom Center (B.C.) Platform, Base(0).

27B. R.Y. I b(B (beta) D / P B 2) - I b(B (beta prime) 5 / P C 2) ;
            U.T.(1)   T.C.(1)   T.L.(1)   T.C.(1)
; II w(Kn A5/Kn A4) X I b(Ki (ganma prime) 4 / Kn (beta prime) 5)).
  B.C.(0)   B.C.(0)   T.L.(1)   T.L.(1)   [END] 3.

In Equation 27B,Sections(A/B),for Section(A),Player I Red-Yellow color band Black Bishop that positions at Row(beta),Column(D),Upper Top(U.T.) section, Base(1), uses the Direct Physical diagonal movement to displace to Row(beta prime), Column(5),Top Left(T.L.) section, Base(1) AND for Section(B),Player I Black Pawn that positions at Row(B),Column (2),Top Center(T.C.) Platform, Base(1),uses the Direct Physical single space horizontal (Chess Set # 4,the Fourth Group having an (A-A) initial position set-up), movement to displace to Row(C),Column(2),Top Center(T.C.) Platform, Base(1).

In Equation 27B,Sections(C/D),for Section(C),Player II Red-Yellow color band (first) White Knight that stations at Row(A),Column(5),*Bottom Center(B.C.) Platform, Base(0),uses the *Direct Abstract 4/2 squares Stealth (silent) [CHECKMATE] attack to capture Player I Black King that positions at Row(gamma prime),Column(4),*Top Left(T.L.) section, Base (1). [END] 3. Player II wins the Red-Yellow color band set. The match continues with the Orange-Blue color band set.

29. O.B. (I w(Kn G1 / P (alpha) D) -   I w(Kn H3 / P 2D) ;
          T.C.(1)   L.B.(0)   T.C.(1)   B.C.(0)
; II b(Kn 8D / Kn 8E) - II b(Kn 6C/ Kn 7H)).
   T.C.(1)   T.C.(1)   T.C.(1)   T.C.(1)

30. O.B. (I w(Q (gamma) E / Kn 1B) - I w(Q (gamma) F / Kn 4A) ;
          L.T.(1)   T.C.(1)   L.B.(0)   T.C.(1)
; II b(P (alpha) B/ P (alpha) E) - II b(P 7B / P 7E)).
   U.B.(0)   U.B.(0)   B.C.(0)   B.C.(0)

31. O.B. (I w(B (alpha) B / Kn 3H) - I w(B (beta) C / Kn (alpha prime) 5) ;
          L.T.(1)   T.C.(1)   L.T.(1)   B.R.(0)
; II b(Kn 7H / P 7B) - II b(Kn 7H)   X
   T.C.(1)   B.C.(0)   T.C.(1)
   X   I w(Kn (alpha prime) 5) / II b(P 7B – P 5B)   ).
          B.R.(0)   B.C.(0)   B.C.(0)

In Equation 31,part 1,Section(A),Player I Orange-Blue color band White Bishop that positions at Row(alpha),Column(B),Lower Top(L.T.) section, Base(1),uses the Direct Physical single space movement to displace to Row(beta),Column(C),Lower Top(L.T.) section, Base(1).

In Equation 31,part 1,Section(B),Player I White Knight that positions at Row(3), Column(H) ,*Top Center(T.C.) Platform, Base(1),uses the *Direct Abstract 3/2 squares movement to displace to Row(alpha prime),Column(5),*Bottom Right(B.R.) section, Base(0).

In Equation 31,part 2,Section(A),Player II Orange-Blue color band Black Knight that stations at Row(7),Column(H),*Top Center(T.C.) Platform, Base(1),uses the *Direct Abstract 3/2 squares attack movement to capture Player I White Knight that positions at Row(alpha prime),Column(5),*Bottom Right(B.R.) section, Base(0).

In Equation 31,part 2,Section(B),Player II Black Pawn that stations at Row(7), Column(B), Bottom Center(B.C.) Platform, Base(0),uses the Direct Physical two spaces movement to displace to Row(5),Column(5),Bottom Center(B.C.) Platform, Base(0).

32. O.B. (I w(B (beta) C) X II b(Kn (alpha prime) 5) - I w(B (alpha prime) 5) ;
          L.T.(1)   B.R.(0)   T.R.(1)
; II b(B (beta) D)   X   I w(B (alpha prime) 5)   ).
   U.B.(0)   T.R.(1)

In Equation 32,part 1,Player I Orange-Blue color band White Bishop that positions at Row(beta),Column(C),*Lower Top(L.T.) section, Base(1),uses the *Direct Abstract diagonal attack movement to capture Player II Black Knight that stations at Row(alpha prime),Column(5),*Bottom Right(B.R.) section, Base(0) and Indirectly LANDS at the corresponding Abstract coordinate of Row(alpha prime),Column(5), *Top Right(T.R.) section, Base(1).

In Equation 32,part 2,Player II Orange-Blue color band Black Bishop that stations at Row (beta),Column(D),*Upper Bottom(U.B.) section, Base(0),uses the *Direct Abstract diagonal attack movement to capture Player I White Bishop that positions at Row(alpha prime),Column(5),*Top Right(T.R.) section, Base(1).

33. O.B. (I w(Kn 4A/ Q (gamma) F) - I w(Kn (alpha prime) 7/ Q (alpha) D) ;
            T.C.(1)   L.T.(1)   B.L.(0)   L.B.(0)

; II b(Kn 6C / P 5B) - II b(Kn 6C) X I w(Kn (alpha prime) 7 /
 T.C.(1)   B.C.(0)   T.C.(1)   B.L.(0)
 / II b(P 5B) X I w(P 4C)).
    B.C.(0)   T.C.(1)

In Equation 33,part 1,Sections(A/B),for Section(A),Player I Orange-Blue color band White Knight that positions at Row(4),Column(A),*Top Center(T.C.) Platform, Base (1),uses the *Direct Abstract 4/2 squares movement to displace to Row(alpha prime) ,Column(7), *Bottom Left(B.L.) section, Base(0) AND for Section(B),Player I White Queen that positions at Row(gamma),Column(F),*Lower Top(L.T.) section, Base (1),uses the *Direct Abstract diagonal movement to displace to Row(alpha),Column (D),*Lower Bottom(L.B.) section, Base(0).

In Equation 33,part 2,Sections(A/B),for Section(A),Player II Orange-Blue color band Black Knight that stations at Row(6),Column(C),*Top Center(T.C.) Platform, Base (1),uses the *Direct Abstract 4/2 squares attack movement to capture Player I White Knight that positions at Row(alpha prime),Column(7),*Bottom Left(B.L.) section, Base(0) AND for Section(B),Player II Black Pawn that stations at Row(5),Column (B),*Bottom Center(B.C.) Platform, Base(0),uses the *Direct Abstract single space diagonal attack movement to capture Player I White Pawn that positions at Row(4), Column(C),*Top Center(T.C.) Platform, Base(1).

34. O.B. (I w(Q (alpha) D) X II b(B (alpha prime) 5) ;
            L.B.(0)   T.R.(1)
 ; II b(Kn (alpha prime) 7 - Kn (beta prime) 4)).
        B.L.(0)   B.L.(0)

In Equation 34,part 1,Player I Orange-Blue color band White Queen that positions at Row(alpha),Column(D),*Lower Bottom(L.B.) section, Base(0),uses the *Direct Abstract diagonal attack movement to capture Player II Black Bishop that stations at Row(alpha prime),Column(5),*Top Right(T.R.) section, Base(1).

In Equation 34,part 2,Player II Orange-Blue color band Black Knight that stations at Row (alpha prime),Column(7),Bottom Left(B.L.) section, Base(0),uses the Direct Physical 4/2 squares movement to displace to Row(beta prime),Column(4),Bottom Left(B.L.) section, Base(0).

35. O.B. (I w(Player I forfeits the turn to play) ;   II b(P 7G - P 6G)).
                                    T.C.(1)   T.C.(1)

36. O.B. (I w(Q (alpha prime) 5) X II b(Ki (gamma) C) ; ....
            T.R.(1)   U.B.(0)   [END] 4.

In Equation 36,part 1,Player I Orange-Blue color band White Queen that positions at Row (alpha prime),Column(5),Top Right(T.R.) section, Base(1),uses the Direct Abstract diagonal Stealth (silent) [CHECKMATE] attack movement to capture Player II Black King that stations at Row(gamma),Column(C),Upper Bottom(U.B.) section, Base(0). Player I wins the Orange-Blue color band set. [END] 4. The match ends with Player I leading Player II with a 3 win victory over Player II out of a possible 4 games.

SECTION B

INCLUDES PHOTOS, DIAGRAMS AND EQUATIONS FOR TRIPLE SET GAME (Q.4.1.1) GAME # 1

Parameters:

1. Pawns may use the two spaces jump movement option in a game.
2. Knights may use either the 3/2 squares or 4/2 squares movement option.
3. Exclusivity - Unique. Meaning NO two pieces of the SAME color band set may have the same Physical AND Abstract squares; this condition leads to a Double Occupancy situation that leaves BOTH pieces vulnerable to a Double capture attack.

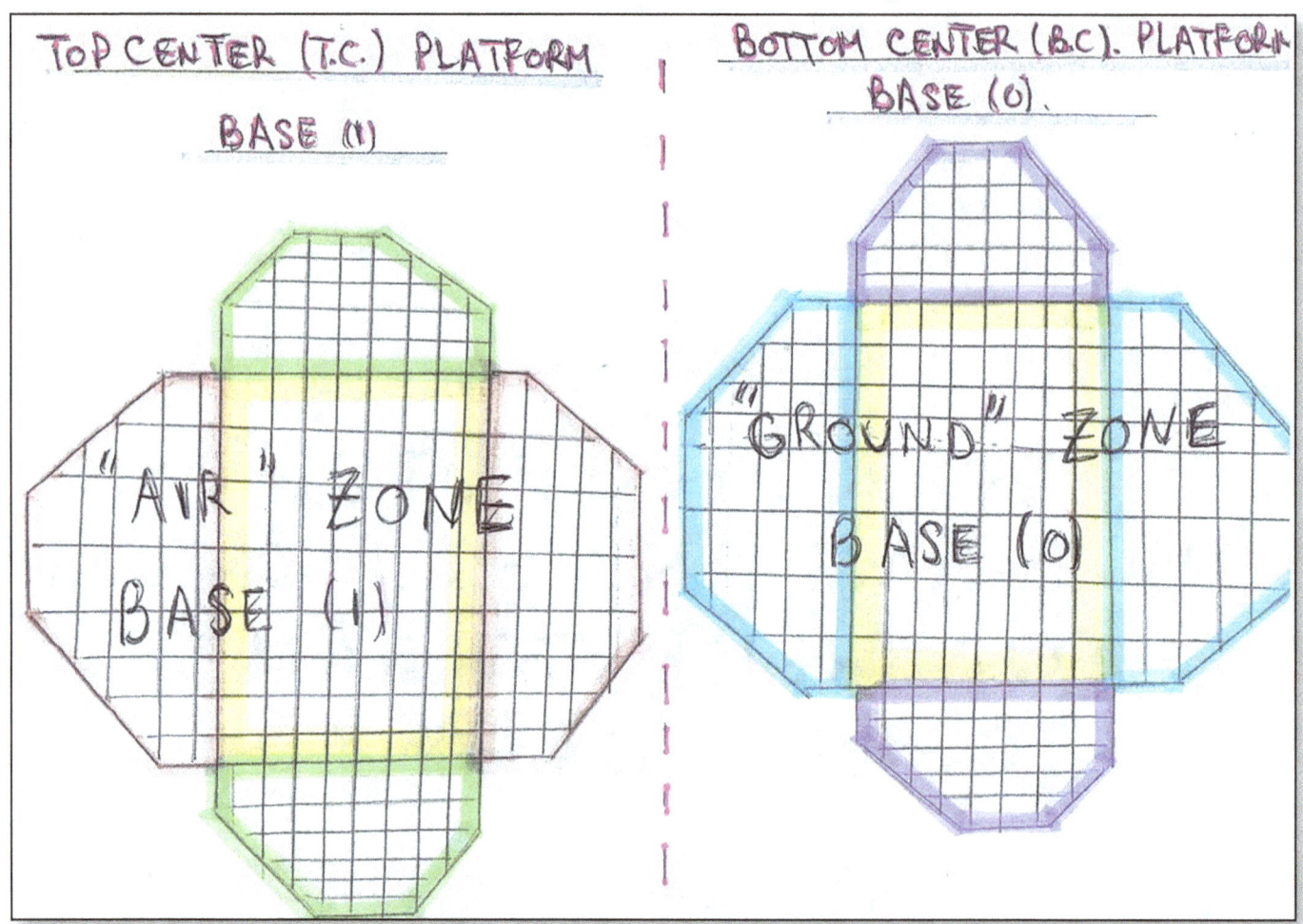

"Diagram 3.5.01 - Indicates the Bottom (GROUND ZONE) Platform at Base (0) and the Top (AIR ZONE) Platform at Base (1). The two Platforms are identical and positions asymmetrically to one another. The Platform closer to you (Player I) is the Top Platform. The Platform further away from you is the Bottom Platform.

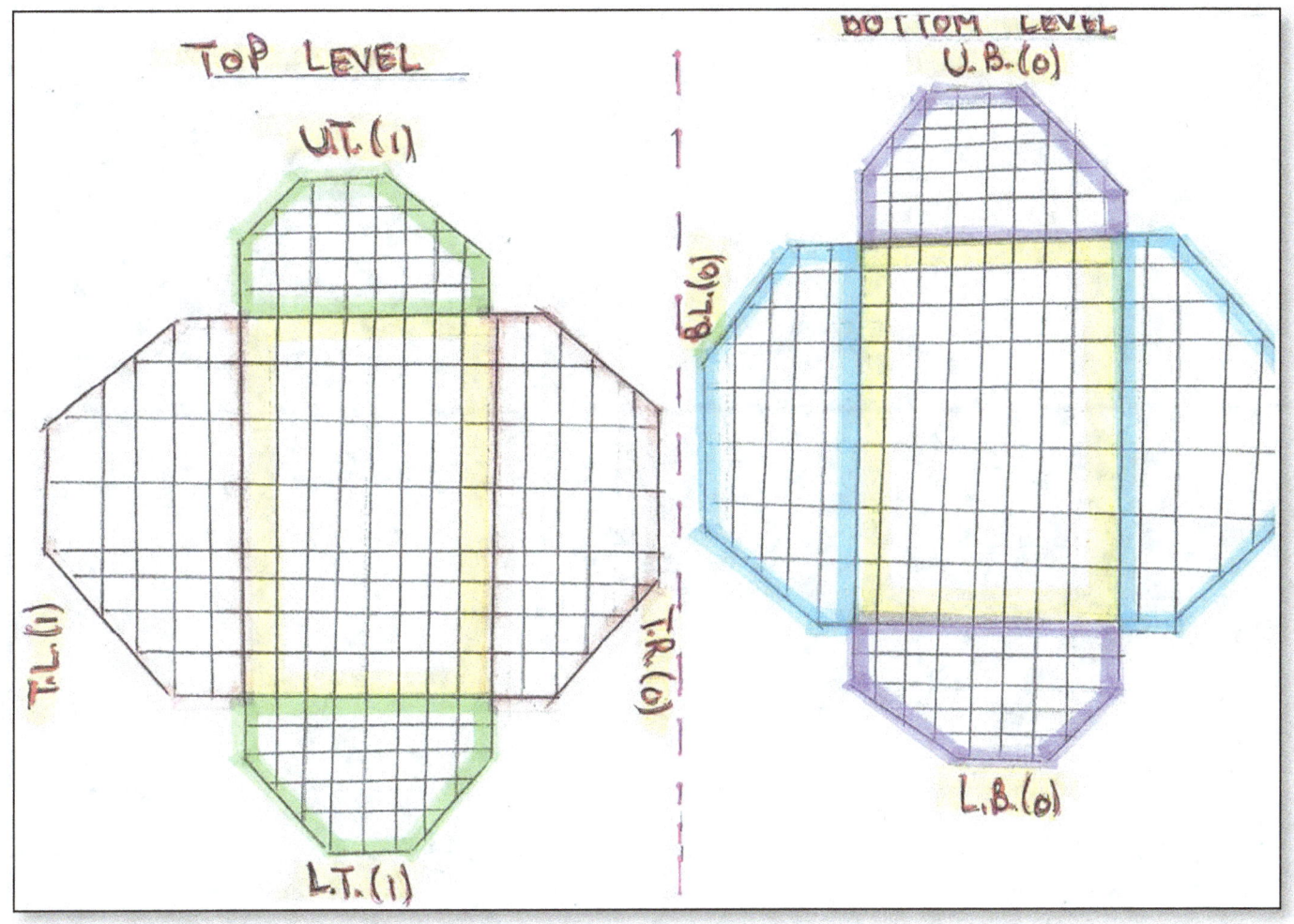

"Diagram 3.5.02 - Presents the Abbreviations for the Sections of the Model."
Left Side: Top Platform (AIR Zone)
L.T.(1)= Lower Top Section at Base (1)
U.T.(1) = Upper Top Section at Base (1)
T.L.(1)= Top Left Section at Base (1)
T.R.(1)=Top Right Section at Base(1).

Right Side: Bottom Platform (GROUND Zone)
L.B.(0)= Lower Bottom Section at Base(0)
U.B.(0)=Upper Bottom Section at Base(0)
B.L.(0)= Bottom Left Section at Base(0)
B.R.(0)=Bottom Right Section at Base(0).

Photo – File 007/# 0878 – This photo shows the initial game boards' set-up. The game board set-up consists of two game boards which are namely the Top (AIR) Platform and the Bottom (GROUND) Platform. The game board that is closer to your view is the Top (AIR) Platform and the game board that is further away is the Bottom (GROUND) Platform. The Top Platform is designated as Base (1) and the Bottom Platform designated as Base (0). The Top Platform has a Center Board to which four Sections are attached; these Sections include the Lower Top (L.T.) section, the Upper Top (U.T.) section, the Top Left (T.L.) section and the Top Right (T.R.) section which are the sections at Base (1). Similarly, the Bottom Platform consists of a Center Board to which four Sections are attached; these Sections include the Lower Bottom (L.B.) section, the Upper Bottom (U.B.) section, the Bottom Left (B.L.) section and the Bottom Right (B.R.) section which are at Base (0). The chess pieces may spontaneously move, position, and capture other chess pieces intermittently between the two Platforms. The Platform upon which a chess piece rests is the Physical Platform and its corresponding asymmetric Platform that is void of any piece is the Abstract Platform. Thus, a chess piece at any given time on the game board may simultaneously attain both a Physical (concrete)position and an Abstract(theoretical)position of which are intrinsically interchangeable and intertwine to the other.

Playing Parameters:

1. The Pawns may use the two spaces movement option beyond the original line of skirmish.
2. The Knights may use either the conventional 3/2 squares movement of the non-conventional 4/2 squares movement.
3. A chess set may not be confined to a single platform field but rather may use both Platforms (the Bottom Platform and the Top Platform) simultaneously, intermittently, and spontaneously.
4. A Player may control three chess sets during a match. The winner of this match must CHECKMATE his/her opponent's Kings thrice. In the case of a tie, a winner may be determined by a win of an additional single set game AFTER the original Double Set game match.
5. The Exclusivity for the chess piece position is Unique. This implies that there is no option for a Double Occupancy, whereby, any two pieces of the same color band set may attain simultaneously BOTH the same Physical square and the same Abstract square at any given instant during a chess engagement. This situation lends itself towards a situation of Double Captivity, thereby exposing both chess pieces in discussion to the vulnerabilities of Double Jeopardy or being Doubled captured (if there is an awareness of this discovery at the time of the removal of any one of the two pieces).
6. The movement of any two pieces of the same color band set, at a time (synchronous Double Movement) is allowed.
7. Players may use the Stealth (silent) [CHECKMATE] capture assault on opponent's(s') Kings.

Folder 21 / # 8812 – Shows the initial position configuration for the Quadruple Set Game (Q.4.1.1) Book 4 Volume 1 Game 1 having a GROUND-TO-GROUND/ GROUND-TO-GROUND/AIR-TO-AIR/ AIR-TO-AIR (G-G)/(G-G)/(A-A)/A-A) initial set-up. Chess set # 1 is the Orange-Blue color band set having a Ground-To-Ground (G-G) initial set-up; the chess pieces move vertically. Chess Set # 2 is the Orange-Red color band set also having a Ground-To-Ground (G-G) initial set-up; the chess pieces move horizontally. Chess Set # 3 is the Red-Purple color band set having an Air-To-Air initial set-up; the chess pieces move vertically. Chess Set # 4 is the Red-Yellow color band set having an (A-A) initial set-up; the chess pieces move horizontally.

Concerning Chess Set # 1, Player I controls the Orange-Blue color band White chess pieces that position at the Lower Bottom (L.B.) section (hexagon), Base (0) of the Bottom (Ground) Platform AND Player II maintains the Orange-Blue color band Black pieces that station at the Upper Bottom (U.B.) section (hexagon), Base (0) also of the Bottom (Ground) Platform. As in conventional chess, the chess pieces move vertically. Chess Set # 1 has a GROUND-TO-GROUND (G-G) initial set-up, thus the first group of letters. This set-up is a Uniform(because Player I and Player II chess pieces are on the SAME Platform which is the Bottom (Ground) Platform), Non-Linear (because the chess pieces position non-linearly) configuration.

With regards to Chess Set # 2, Player I controls the Orange-Red color band Black chess pieces that position at the Bottom Left (B.L.) section (hexagon), Base(0) of the Bottom (Ground) Platform AND Player II maintains the Orange-Red color band White chess pieces that station at Bottom Right (B.R.) section (hexagon), Base (0) also of the Bottom (Ground) Platform. Contrary to conventional chess, the chess pieces move horizontally. Chess Set # 2 has a GROUND-TO-GROUND (G-G) initial set-up, thus the second group of letters. This set-up is also a Uniform, Non-Linear configuration.

Folder 21/ # 8813 – Presents the initial position set-up for the chess pieces for the Quadruple Game (Q.4.1.1) Book 4 Volume 1 Game 1. This photo also shows the Position BEFORE the Displacement (P.B.D.) of the chess pieces for Equation 1.

Considering Chess Set # 3, Player I controls the Red-Purple color band White chess pieces that position at the Lower Top (L.T.) section (hexagon), Base (1) of the Top (Air) Platform AND Player II maintains the Red-Purple color band Black chess pieces that station at the Upper Top (U.T.) section (hexagon), Base(1) also of the Top (Air) Platform. Like conventional chess, the chess pieces move vertically. Chess Set # 3 has an AIR-TO-AIR (A-A) initial set-up, thus the third group of letters. This set-up is a Uniform, non-Linear configuration.

Regarding Chess Set # 4, Player I controls the Red-Yellow color band Black chess pieces that position at the Top Left (T.L.) section (hexagon), Base (1) of the Top (Air) Platform AND Player II maintains the Red-Yellow color band White chess pieces that station at the Top Right (T.R.) section (hexagon), Base (1) also of the Top (Air) Platform. Unlike conventional chess, the chess pieces move horizontally. Chess Set # 4 has an AIR-TO-AIR (A-A) initial set-up, thus the fourth group of letters. This set-up is a Uniform (because Player I and Player II chess pieces are on the SAME Platform, the Top (Air) Platform), non-Linear (because the chess pieces are positioned non-linearly) configuration.

Folder 21 / # 8814 – Demonstrates the Position AFTER the Displacement (P.A.D.) of the chess pieces for Equation 1.

1. R.Y. (I b(P (alpha prime) 2 / P (alpha prime) 7 - I b(P B2 / P B7) ;
            T.L.(1)   T.L.(1)   T.C.(1)   T.C.(1)
; II w(P (alpha prime) 1 / P (alpha prime) 8 - II w(P G1 / P G8)).
    T.R.(1)   T.R.(1)   B.C.(0)   B.C.(0)

In Equation 1,part 1,Sections(A/B),for Section(A),Player I (first) Red-Yellow color band Black Pawn that previously positioned at Row(alpha prime),Column(2),Top Left(T.L.) section, Base(1),uses the Direct Physical two spaces(unto the second immediate available vacant square) <u>horizontal</u> (Chess Set # 4,the Fourth Group of letters, having an (A-A) initial position set-up) movement to displace to Row(B), Column(2),Top Center(T.C.) Platform, Base(1) AND for Section (B),Player I (second) Red-Yellow color band Black Pawn that previously positioned at Row(alpha prime),Column(7),Top Left(T.L.) section, Base(1),also uses the Direct Physical two spaces movement to displace to Row(B),Column(7), Top Center(T.C.) Platform, Base(1).

In Equation 1,part 2,Sections(C/D),for Section(C),Player II (first) Red-Yellow color band White Pawn that previously stationed at Row(alpha prime),Column(1),Top Right(T.R.) section, Base(1),uses the Direct Abstract two spaces <u>horizontal</u> movement to displace to Row(G),Column(1),Bottom Center(B.C.) Platform, Base(0) AND for Section(D),Player II (second) White Pawn that previously stationed at Row(alpha prime),Column(8),Top Right(T.R.) section, Base(1),also uses the Direct Abstract two spaces movement to displace to Row(G),Column(8),Bottom Center (B.C.) Platform, Base(0).

Folder 21 / # 8815 – Examines the Position BEFORE the Displacement (P.B.D.) of the chess pieces in Equation 2.

2. R.P. (I w(P (alpha) B / P (alpha) G   - I w(P 3B / P 3G) ;
             L.T.(1)   L.T.(1)   T.C.(1)   B.C.(0)
  ; II b(P (alpha) B / P (alpha) G   -   II b(P 6B / P 6G)   ).
     U.T.(1)   U.T.(1)   T.C.(1)   B.C.(0)

Folder 21/ # 8816 – Examines the Position AFTER the Displacement (P.A.D.) of the chess pieces for Equation 2.

2. R.P. (I w(P (alpha) B / P (alpha) G - I w(P 3B/ P 3G) ;
            L.T.(1)   L.T.(1)   T.C.(1)   B.C.(0)
; II b(P (alpha) B / P (alpha) G - II b(P 6B / P 6G)).
        U.T.(1)   U.T.(1)   T.C.(1)   B.C.(0)

In Equation 2,part 1,Sections(A/B),for Section(A),Player I (first) Red-Purple color band White Pawn that previously positioned at Row(alpha),Column(B),Lower Top(L.T.) section, Base(1),uses the Direct Physical two spaces <u>vertical</u> (Chess Set # 3,the Third Group of letters, having an (A-A) initial position set-up) movement (unto to second immediate available vacant square) to displace to Row(3),Column(B),Top Center(T.C.) Platform, Base(1) AND for Section(B),Player I (second) White Pawn that previously positioned at Row(alpha), Column (G),*Lower Top(L.T.) section, Base(1),uses the *Direct Abstract two spaces movement to displace to Row(3), Column(G), *Bottom Center(B.C.) Platform, Base(0).

In Equation 2,part 2,Sections(C/D),for Section(C),Player II (first) Red-Purple color band Black Pawn that previously stationed at Row(alpha),Column(B),Upper Top (U.T.) section, Base(1),uses the Direct Physical two spaces <u>vertical</u> movement to displace to Row(6), Column(B),Top Center(T.C.) Platform, Base(1) AND for Section(D),Player II (second) Black Pawn that previously stationed at Row(alpha), Column(G),*Upper Top(U.T.) section, Base(1),uses the *Direct Abstract two spaces movement to displace to Row (6),Column(G),*Bottom Center(B.C.) Platform, Base(0).

Folder 21 / # 8817 - Demonstrates the Position BEFORE the Displacement (P.B.D.) of the chess pieces for Equation 3.

3. O.R. (I b(P (alpha prime) 2 / P (alpha prime) 3 - I b(P C2 / P C3) ;
                B.L.(0)   B.L.(0)   T.C.(1)   T.C.(1)
 ; II w(P (alpha prime) 1 / P (alpha prime) 8 - II w(P F1 / P F8)).
    B.R.(0)   B.R.(0)   B.C.(0)   B.C.(0)

Folder 21 / # 8818 - Reveals the Position AFTER the Displacement (P.A.D.) of the chess pieces for Equation 3.

3. O.R. (I b(P (alpha prime) 2 / P (alpha prime) 3 - I b(P C2 / P C3) ;
             B.L.(0)   B.L.(0)   T.C.(1)   T.C.(1)
; II w(P (alpha prime) 1 / P (alpha prime) 8 - II w(P F1 / P F8)).
   B.R.(0)   B.R.(0)   B.C.(0)   B.C.(0)

In Equation 3,part 1,Sections(A/B),for Section(A),Player I (first) Orange-Red color band Black Pawn that previously positioned at Row(alpha prime),Column(2), *Bottom Left(B.L.) section, Base(0),uses the *Direct Abstract two spaces <u>horizontal</u> (Chess Set # 2, the Second Group of letters, having a (G-G) initial position set-up) movement to displace to Row(C),Column(2), *Top Center(T.C.) Platform, Base(1) AND for Section(B),Player I (second) Black Pawn that previously positioned at Row(alpha prime), Column(3),*Bottom Left(B.L.) section, Base(0), also uses the *Direct Abstract two spaces movement (unto the second immediate available vacant square) to displace to Row(C),Column(3),*Top Center (T.C.) Platform, Base(1).

In Equation 3,part 2,Sections(C/D), for Section(C),Player II (first) Orange-Red color band White Pawn that previously stationed at Row(alpha prime),Column(1),Bottom Right(B.R.) section, Base(0),uses the Direct Physical two spaces <u>horizontal</u> movement (unto the second immediate available vacant square) to displace to Row (F),Column(1),Bottom Center(B.C.) Platform, Base(0) AND for Section(D), Player II (second) White Pawn that previously stationed at Row(alpha prime),Column(8),Bottom Right(B.R.) section, Base(0), also uses the Direct Physical two spaces movement to displace to Row(F),Column (8),Bottom Center(B.C.) Platform, Base(0).

Folder 21 / # 8819 - Explains the Position BEFORE the Displacement (P.B.D.) of the chess pieces for Equation 4.

4. O.B. (I w(P (alpha) B / P (alpha) C   - I w(P 4B / P 4C) ;
              L.B.(0)   L.B.(0)   T.C.(1)   T.C.(1)
; II b(P (alpha) F / P (alpha) G   - II b(P 7F / P 7G)).
     U.B.(0)   U.B.(0)   T.C.(1)   T.C.(1)

Folder 21 / # 8820 - Reveals the Position AFTER the Displacement (P.A.D.) of the chess pieces for Equation 4.

4. O.B. (I w(P (alpha) B / P (alpha) C - I w(P 4B / P 4C) ;
           L.B.(0)   L.B.(0)   T.C.(1)   T.C.(1)
; II b(P (alpha) F / P (alpha) G - II b(P 7F / P 7G)).
    U.B.(0)   U.B.(0)   T.C.(1)   T.C.(1)

In Equation 4,part 1,Sections(A/B),for Section(A),Player I (first) Orange-Blue color band White Pawn that previously positioned at Row(alpha),Column(B),*Lower Bottom(L.B.) section, Base(0),uses the *Direct Abstract two spaces <u>vertical</u> (Chess Set # 1,the First Group of letters, having a (G-G) initial position set-up) movement (unto the second immediate available vacant square) to displace to Row(4),Column (B),*Top center (T.C.) Platform, Base(1) AND for Section(B),Player I (second) White Pawn that previously positioned at Row(alpha),Column (C),*Lower Bottom (L.B.) section, Base(0),also uses the *Direct Abstract two spaces movement to displace to Row(4),Column(C),*Top Center(T.C.) Platform, Base(1).

In Equation 4,part 2,Sections(C/D),for Section(C),Player II (first) Orange-Blue color band Black Pawn that previously stationed at Row(alpha),Column(F),*Upper Bottom(U.B.) section, Base(0),uses the *Direct Abstract two spaces <u>vertical</u> movement to displace to Row(7),Column(F),*Top Center(T.C.) Platform, Base(1) AND for Sections(D), Player II (second) Black Pawn that previously stationed at Row(alpha),Column(G),*Upper Bottom(U.B.) section, Base(0),also uses the *Direct Abstract two spaces movement to displace to Row(7),Column(G),*Top Center(T.C.) Platform, Base(1).

Folder 21 / # 8821 - Unveils the Position BEFORE the Displacement (P.B.D.) of the chess pieces for Equation 5.

5. R.Y.   (I b(P (alpha prime) 3 / P (alpha prime) 4 - I b(P D3 / P D4) ;
                    T.L.(1)   T.L.(1)   T.C.(1)   T.C.(1)
; II w(P (alpha prime) 3 / P (alpha prime) 6 - II w(P F3 / P F6)).
        T.R.(1)   T.R.(1)   B.C.(0)   B.C.(0)

Folder 21 / # 8822 - Represents the Position AFTER the Displacement (P.A.D.) of the chess pieces for Equation 5.

5. R.Y.   (I b(P (alpha prime) 3/ P (alpha prime) 4 - I b(P D3 / P D4) ;
                    T.L.(1)   T.L.(1)   T.C.(1)   T.C.(1)
; II w(P (alpha prime) 3 / P (alpha prime) 6 - II w(P F3 / P F6)).
         T.R.(1)   T.R.(1)   B.C.(0)   B.C.(0)

In Equation 5,part 1,Sections(A/B),for Section(A),Player I (first) Red-Yellow color band Black Pawn that previously positioned at Row(alpha prime),Column(3),Top Left(T.L.) section, Base(1),uses the Direct Physical two spaces <u>horizontal</u> (Chess Set # 4,the Fourth Group of letters, having an (A-A) initial position configuration) movement (unto the second immediate available vacant square) to displace to Row (D),Column (3),Top Center(T.C.) Platform, Base(1) AND for Section(B),Player I (second) Black Pawn that previously positioned at Row(alpha prime),Column(4),Top Left(T.L.) section, Base(1), also uses the Direct Physical two spaces movement to displace to Row(D),Column (4),Top Center(T.C.) Platform, Base(1).

In Equation 5,part 2,Sections(C/D),for Section(C),Player II (first) Red-Yellow color band White Pawn that previously stationed at Row(alpha prime),Column(3),*Top Right(T.R.) section, Base(1),uses the *Direct Abstract two spaces <u>horizontal</u> movement to displace to Row(F),Column(3),*Bottom Center(B.C.) Platform, Base(0) AND for Section(D), Player II (second) White Pawn that previously stationed at Row(alpha prime), Column(6),*Top Right(T.R.) section, Base(1),also uses the *Direct Abstract two spaces movement to displace to Row(F),Column(6),*Bottom Center(B.C.) Platform, Base(0).

Folder 21 / # 8823 - Illustrates the Position BEFORE the Displacement (P.B.D.) of the chess pieces for Equation 6.

6. R.P.   (I w(P (alpha) A / P (alpha) C   - I w(P 2A / P 2C   ) ;
              L.T.(1)   L.T(1)   B.C.(0)   B.C.(0)
 ; II b(P (alpha) F / P (alpha) H   -   II b(P 7F / P 7H   )   ).
      U.T.(1)   U.T.(1)   B.C.(0)   T.C.(1)

Folder 22 / # 8824 – Presents the Position AFTER the Displacement (P.A.D.) of the chess pieces in Equation 6.

6. R.P. (I w(P (alpha) A / P (alpha) C - I w(P 2A / P 2C) ;
   L.T.(1)   L.T.(1)   B.C.(0)   B.C.(0)
; II b(P (alpha) F / P (alpha) H - II b(P 7F / P 7H)).
 U.T.(1)   U.T.(1)   B.C.(0)   T.C.(1)

In Equation 6,part 1,Sections(A/B),for Section(A),Player I (first) Red-Purple band White Pawn that previously positioned at Row(alpha),Column(A),*Lower Top(L.T.) section, Base(1),uses the *Direct Abstract two spaces <u>vertical</u> (Chess Set # 3,the Third group of letters, having an (A-A) initial position set-up) movement to displace to Row(2), Column(A),*Bottom Center(B.C.) Platform, Base(0) AND for Section(B), Player I (second) White Pawn that previously positioned at Row(alpha),Column(C), *Lower Top(L.T.) section, Base(1),uses the *Direct Abstract two spaces movement to displace to Row (2),Column(C),*Bottom Center(B.C.) Platform, Base(0).

In Equation 6,part 2,Sections(C/D),for Section(D),Player II (first) Red-Purple color band Black Pawn that previously stationed at Row(alpha),Column(F),*Upper Top (U.T.) section, Base(1),uses the *Direct Abstract two spaces <u>vertical</u> movement to displace to Row (7),Column(F),*Bottom Center(B.C.) Platform, Base(0) AND for Section(D), Player II (second) Black Pawn that previously stationed at Row(alpha), Column(H),Upper Top(U.T.) section, Base(1),uses the Direct Physical two spaces movement to displace to Row (7),Column(H),Top Center(T.C.) Platform, Base(1).

Folder 22 / # 8825 – Shows the Position BEFORE the Displacement (P.B.D.) of the chess pieces for Equation 7.

7. O.R. (I b(P (alpha prime) 7 / P (alpha prime) 8 - I b(P B7 / P B8) ;
                    B.L.(0)   B.L.(0)   B.C.(0)   B.C.(0)
  ; II w(P (alpha prime) 3 / P (alpha prime) 7 - I w(P E3 / P E7)   ).
        B.R.(0)   B.R.(0)   B.C.(0)   T.C.(1)

Folder 22 / # 8826 - Displays the Position AFTER the Displacement (P.A.D.) of the chess pieces for Equation 7.

7. O.R.   (I b(P (alpha prime) 7 / P (alpha prime) 8 - I b(P B7 / P B8   ) ;
              B.L.(0)   B.L.(0)   B.C.(0)   B.C.(0)
; II w(P (alpha prime) 3 / P (alpha prime) 7 - II w(P E3 / P E7)).
     B.R.(0)   B.R.(0)   B.C.(0)   T.C.(1)

In Equation 7,part 1,Sections(A/B),for Section(A),Player I (first) Orange-Red color band Black Pawn that previously positioned at Row(alpha prime),Column(7),Bottom Left(B.L.) section, Base(0),uses the Direct Physical two spaces <u>horizontal</u> (Chess Set # 2, the Second Group of letters, having an (A-A) initial position configuration) movement to displace to Row(B),Column(7),Bottom Center(B.C.) Platform, Base(0) AND for Section(B),Player I (second) Black Pawn that previously positioned at Row(alpha prime),Column (8),Bottom Left(B.L.) section, Base(0),also uses the Direct Physical two spaces movement to displace to Row(B),Column(8),Bottom Center(B.C.) Platform, Base(0).

In Equation 7,part 2,Sections(C/D),for Section(C),Player II (first) Orange-Red color band White Pawn that previously stationed at Row(alpha prime),Column(3),Bottom Right(B.R.) section, Base(0),uses the Direct Physical two spaces <u>horizontal</u> movement to displace to Row(E),Column(3), Bottom Center(B.C.) Platform, Base(0) AND for Section(D), Player II (second) White Pawn that previously stationed at Row(alpha prime),Column (7), *Bottom Right(B.R.) section, Base(0),uses the *Direct Abstract two spaces movement to displace to Row(E),Column(7),*Top Center(T.C.) Platform, Base(1).

Folder 22 / # 8827 – Explains the Position BEFORE the Displacement (P.B.D.) of the chess pieces for Equation 8.

8. O.B. (I w(P (alpha) F / P (alpha) G - I w(P 4F / P 4G)) ;
           L.B.(0)   L.B.(0)   B.C.(0)   B.C.(0)
 ; II b(P (alpha) C / P (alpha) D - II b(P 7C / P 7D)).
       U.B.(0)   U.B.(0)   B.C.(0)   B.C.(0)

Folder 22 / # 8828 - Illustrates the Position AFTER the Displacement (P.A.D.) of the chess pieces for Equation 8.

8. O.B.   (I w(P (alpha) F / P (alpha) G - I w(P 4F / P 4G)   ;
            L.B.(0)   L.B.(0)   B.C.(0)   B.C.(0)
; II b(P (alpha) C / P (alpha) D   - II b(P 7C / P 7D)).
      U.B.(0)   U.B.(0)   B.C.(0)   B.C.(0)

In Equation 8,part 1,Sections(A/B),for Section(A),Player I (first) Orange-Blue color band White Pawn that previously positioned at Row(alpha),Column(F),Lower Bottom(L.B.) section, Base(0),uses the Direct Physical two spaces two spaces <u>vertical</u> (Chess Set # 1,having a (G-G) initial position set-up) movement to displace to Row(4),Column (F),Bottom Center(B.C) Platform, Base(0) AND for Section(B), Player I (second) White Pawn that previously positioned at Row(alpha),Column (G), Lower Bottom(L.B.) section, Base(0),uses the Direct Physical two spaces movement to displace to Row(4), Column(G),Bottom Center(B.C.) Platform, Base(0).

In Equation 8,part 2,Sections(C/D),for Section(C),Player II (first) Orange-Blue color band Black Pawn that previously stationed at Row(alpha),Column(C),Upper Bottom(U.B.) section, Base(0),uses the Direct Physical two spaces <u>vertical</u> movement to displace to Row(7),Column(C),Bottom Center(B.C.) Platform, Base(0) AND for Section(D), Player II (second) Black Pawn that previously stationed at Row (alpha),Column(D),Upper Bottom(U.B.) section, Base(0),uses the Direct Physical two spaces movement to displace to Row(7),Column(D),Bottom Center(B.C.) Platform, Base(0).

Folder 22 / # 8829 – Presents the Position BEFORE the Displacement (P.B.D.) of the chess pieces for Equation 9.

9. R.Y. (I b(P (alpha prime) 5/ P (alpha prime) 6 - I b(P B5 / P B6) ;
                T.L.(1)   T.L.(1)   B.C.(0)   B.C.(0)
; II w(Kn (gamma prime) 3 / Kn (gamma prime) 6 - II w(Kn H4 / Kn H5)).
        T.R.(1)   T.R.(1)   T.C.(1)   T.C.(1)

Folder 22 / # 8830 – Examines the Position AFTER the Displacement (P.A.D.) of the chess pieces for Equation 9.

9. R.Y.   (I b(P (alpha prime) 5 / P (alpha prime) 6 - I b(P B5 / P B6)   ;
            T.L.(1)   T.L.(1)   B.C.(0)   B.C.(0)
; II w(Kn (gamma prime) 3 / Kn (gamma prime) 6 - II w(Kn H4 / Kn H5)).
      T.R.(1)   T.R.(1)   T.C.(1)   T.C.(1)

In Equation 9,part 1,Sections(A/B),for Section(A),Player I (first) Red-Purple color band Black Pawn that previously positioned at Row(alpha prime),Column(5),*Top Left(T.L.) section, Base(1),uses the *Direct Abstract two spaces <u>horizontal</u> (Chess Set # 4,the Fourth Group of letters, having an (A-A) initial position set-up) movement (unto the immediate second available vacant square) to displace to Row(B),Column(5), *Bottom Center(B.C.) Platform, Base(0) AND for Section(B),Player I (second) Black Pawn that previously positioned at Row(alpha prime),Column(6),*Top Left(T.L.) section, Base (1),also uses the* Direct Abstract two spaces movement to displace to Row(B), Column(6), *Bottom Center(B.C.) Platform, Base(0).

In Equation 9,part 2,Sections(C/D),for Section(C),Player II (first) Red-Yellow color band White Knight that previously stationed at Row(gamma prime),Column(3),Top Right(T.R.) section, Base(1),uses the Direct Physical 4/2 squares movement to displace to Row (H),Column(4),Top Center(T.C.) Platform, Base(1) AND for Section(D),Player II (second) White Knight that previously stationed at Row(gamma prime), Column(6),Top Right (T.R.) section, Base(1),also uses the Direct Physical 4/2 squares movement to displace to Row(H),Column(5),Top Center(T.C.) Platform, Base(1).

Folder 22 / # 8831 – Reveals the Position BEFORE the Displacement (P.B.D.) of the chess pieces for Equation 10.

10. R.P. (I w(P (alpha) F / P (alpha) H - I w(P 2F / P 2H) ;
            L.T.(1)   L.T.(1)   T.C.(1)   T.C.(1)
; II b(P (alpha) C / P (alpha) D - II b(P 6C / P 6D)).
    U.T.(1)   U.T.(1)   B.C.(0)   B.C.(0)

Folder 22 / # 8832 – Displays the Position AFTER the Displacement (P.A.D.) of the chess pieces for Equation 10.

10. R.P. (I w(P (alpha) F / P (alpha) H - I w (P 2F/ P 2H) ;
        L.T.(1)   L.T.(1)   T.C.(1)   T.C.(1)
; II b(P (alpha) C / P (alpha) D   - II b(P 6C / P 6D)).
   U.T.(1)   U.T.(1)   B.C.(0)   B.C.(0)

In Equation 10, part 1, Sections (A/B), for Section(A), Player I (first) Red-Purple color band White Pawn that previously positioned at Row(alpha), Column(F), Lower Top(L.T.) section, Base(1), uses the Direct Physical two spaces <u>vertical</u> (Chess Set # 3, the Third Group of letters, having an (A-A) initial position configuration) movement to displace to Row(2), Column(F), Top Center(T.C.) Platform, Base(1) AND for Section(B), Player I (second) White Pawn that previously positioned at Row(alpha), Column(H), Lower Top(L.T.) section, Base(1), also uses the Direct Physical two spaces movement to displace to Row(2), Column(H), Top Center(T.C.) Platform, Base(1).

In Equation 10, part 2, Sections(C/D), for Section(C), Player II (first) Red-Purple color band Black Pawn that previously stationed at Row(alpha), Column(C), *Upper Top (U.T.) section, Base(1), uses the *Direct Abstract two spaces <u>vertical</u> movement to displace to Row (6), Column(C), *Bottom Center(B.C.) Platform, Base(0) AND for Section(D), Player II (second) Black Pawn that previously stationed at Row(alpha), Column(D), *Upper Top(U.T.) section, Base(1), also uses the *Direct Abstract two spaces movement to displace to Row(6), Column(D), *Bottom Center(B.C.) Platform, Base(0).

Folder 22 / # 8833 – Depicts the Position BEFORE the Displacement (P.B.D.) of the chess piece for Equation 11.

11. O.R. (I b(P (alpha prime) 4 / P (alpha prime) 5 - I b (P B4 / P C5) ;
                B.L.(0)   B.L.(0)   B.C.(0)   B.C.(0)
; II w(P (alpha prime) 2 / P (alpha prime) 6   - II w (P E 2 / P E 6)).
      B.R.(0)   B.R.(0)   T.C.(1)   B.C.(0)

Folder 22 / # 8834 – Illustrates the Position AFTER the Displacement (P.A.D.) of the chess pieces for Equation 11.

11. O.R.   (I b(P (alpha prime) 4 /P (alpha prime) 5 - I b(P B4 / P C5) ;
         B.L.(0)   B.L.(0)   B.C.(0)   B.C.(0)
; II w(P (alpha prime) 2 / P (alpha prime) 6 - II w(P E 2 / P E 6)).
     B.R.(0)   B.R.(0)   T.C.(1)   B.C.(0)

In Equation 11, part 1, Sections(A/B), for Section(A), Player I (first) Orange-Red color band Black Pawn that previously positioned at Row(alpha prime), Column(4), Bottom Left(B.L.) section, Base(0), uses the Direct Physical two spaces <u>horizontal</u> (Chess Set # 2, the Second Group, having a (G-G) initial position set-up) movement (unto the immediate second available vacant square) to displace to Row(B), Column(4), Bottom Center(B.C.) Platform, Base(0) AND for Section(B), Player I (second) Black Pawn that previously positioned at Row(alpha prime), Column(5), Bottom Left(B.L.) section, Base(0), also uses the Direct Physical two space movement (unto the second immediate available vacant square) to displace to Row(C), Column(5), Bottom Left(B.L.) section, Base(0).

In Equation 11, part 2, Sections(C/D), for Section(C), Player II (first) Orange-Red color band White Pawn that previously stationed at Row(alpha prime), Column(2), Bottom Right(B.R.) section, Base(0), uses the Direct Abstract two spaces <u>horizontal</u> movement to displace to Row(E), Column(2), Top Center(T.C.) Platform, Base(1) AND for Section (D), Player II (second) White Pawn that previously stationed at Row(alpha prime), Column(6), Bottom Right(B.R.) section, Base(0), uses the Direct Physical two spaces movement to displace to Row(E), Column(6), Bottom Center(B.C.) Platform, Base(0).

Folder 22 / # 8835 – Unveils the Position BEFORE the Displacement (P.B.D.) of the chess pieces for Equation 12.

12. O.B. (I w(B (gamma) D/B (gamma) E - I w(B (alpha) B/B (alpha) G) ;
          L.B.(0)   L.B.(0)   L.T.(1)   L.T.(1)
; II b(B (gamma) D / B (gamma) E - II b(B (beta) E / B (beta) D   )   ).
   U.B.(0)   U.B.(0)   U.B.(0)   U.B.(0)

Folder 22 / # 8836 – Demonstrates the Position AFTER the Displacement (P.A.D.) of the chess pieces for Equation 12.

12.   O.B. (I w(B(gamma) D/B (gamma) E - I w(B (alpha) B/B (alpha) G ;
                L.B.(0)   L.B.(0)   L.T.(1)   L.T.(1)
; II b(B (gamma) D / B (gamma) E   - II b(B (beta) E / B (beta) D)).
     U.B.(0)   U.B.(0)   U.B.(0)   U.B.(0)

In equation 12,part 1,Sections(A/B),for Section(A),Player I (first) Orange-Blue color band White Bishop that previously positioned at Row(gamma),Column(D),Lower Bottom(L.B.) section, Base(0),uses the Direct Abstract diagonal movement to displace to Row (alpha),Column(B),Lower Top(L.T.) section, Base(1) AND for Section(B),Player I (second) White Bishop that previously positioned at Row (gamma),Column(E),Lower Bottom (L.B.) section, Base(0),also uses the Direct Abstract diagonal movement to displace to Row(alpha),Column(G),Lower Top(L.T.) section, Base(1).

In Equation 12,part 2,Sections(C/D),for Section(C),Player II (first) Orange-Blue color band Black Bishop that previously stationed at Row(gamma),Column(D), Upper Bottom (U.B.) section, Base(0),uses the Direct Physical diagonal movement to displace to Row(beta),Column(E),Upper Bottom(U.B.) section, Base(0) AND for Section(D) ,Player II (second) Black Bishop that previously stationed at Row (gamma),Column(E),Upper Bottom(U.B.) section, Base(0),also uses the Direct Physical diagonal movement to displace to Row(beta),Column(D),Upper Bottom(U.B.) section, Base(0).

Folder 22 / # 8837 – Explains the Position BEFORE the Displacement (P.B.D.) of the chess pieces for Equation 13.

13. R.Y.   (I b(B (gamma prime) 4 / B (gamma prime) 5 -
                 T.L.(1)   T.L.(1)
     - I b(B (beta) D / B (beta) C   ;
          U.T.(1)   U.T.(1)
  ; II w(P G1 / P G8)   -   II w(P D1 / P D8)   ).
    B.C.(0)   B.C.(0)   B.C.(0)   B.C.(0)

Folder 21 / # 8838 - Presents the Position AFTER the Displacement (P.A.D.) of the chess pieces for Equation 13.

13. R.Y. (I b(B (gamma prime) 4 / B (gamma prime) 5 -
                    T.L.(1)   T.L.(1)
  - I b(B (beta) D / B (beta) C ;
        U.T.(1)   U.T.(1)
;   II w(P G1 / P G8) - II w(P D1 / P D8)   ).
    B.C.(0)   B.C.(0)   B.C.(0)   B.C.(0)

In Equation 13,part 1,Sections(A/B),for Section(A),Player I (first) Red-Yellow color band Black Bishop that previously positioned at Row(gamma prime),Column(4),Top Left(T.L.) section, Base(1),uses the Direct Physical diagonal movement to displace to Row (beta),Column(D),Upper Top(U.T.) section, Base(1) AND for Section(B), Player I (second) Black Bishop that previously positioned at Row(gamma prime), Column(5),Top Left (T.L.) section, Base(1),also uses the Direct Physical diagonal movement to displace to Row(beta),Column(C),Upper Top(U.T.) section, Base(1).

In Equation 13,part 2,Sections(C/D),for Section(C),Player II (first) Red-Yellow color band White Pawn that previously stationed at Row(G),Column(1),Bottom Center (B.C.) Platform, Base(0),uses the Direct Physical two spaces horizontal (Chess Set # 4,the Fourth Group of letters, having an (A-A) initial position set-up) movement to displace to Row(D),Column(1),Bottom Center(B.C.) Platform, Base(0) AND for Section(D), Player II (second) White Pawn that previously stationed at Row(G), Column(8),Bottom Center (B.C.) Platform, Base(0),also uses the Direct Physical two spaces movement to displace to Row(D),Column(8),Bottom Center(B.C.) Platform, Base(0).

Folder 21 / # 8839 – Discloses the Position BEFORE the Displacement (P.B.D.) of the chess pieces for Equation 14.

14. R.P. (I w(B (gamma) D / B (gamma) E - I w(B (beta) E / B (beta) D ;
           L.T.(1)   L.T.(1)   L.B.(0)   L.B.(0)
; II b(C (beta) B / C (beta) G -   II b(C 8B / C 8G)).
  U.T.(1)   U.T.(1)   T.C.(1)   T.C.(1)

Folder 21 / # 8840 – Demonstrates the Position AFTER the Displacement (P.A.D.) of the chess pieces for Equation 14.

14. R.P. (I w(B (gamma) D / B (gamma) E - I w(B (beta) E / B (beta) D ;
　　　　　　　L.T.(1)　　　　　L.T.(1)　　　　L.B.(0)　　　　L.B.(0)
; II b(C (beta) B / C (beta) G - II b(C 8B / C 8G)).
　　U.T.(1)　　　　U.T.(1)　　　T.C.(1)　　　T.C.(1)

In Equation 14,part 1,Sections(A/B),for Section(A),Player I (first) Red-Purple color band White Bishop that previously positioned at Row(gamma),Column(D),*Lower Top(L.T.) section, Base(1),uses the *Direct Abstract diagonal movement to displace to Row (beta),Column(E),*Lower Bottom(L.B.) section, Base(0) AND for Section (B),Player I (second) White Bishop that previously positioned at Row(gamma), Column(E),*Lower Top (L.T.) section, Base(1),also uses the *Direct Abstract diagonal movement to displace to Row(beta),Column(D),*Lower Bottom(L.B.) section, Base(0).

In Equation 14,part 2,Sections(C/D),for Section(C),Player II (first) Red-Purple color band Black Castle that previously stationed at Row(beta),Column(B),Upper Top (U.T.) section, Base(1),uses the Direct Physical movement to displace to Row(8), Column(B),Top Center(T.C.) Platform, Base(1) AND for Section(D),Player II (second) Black Castle that previously stationed at Row(beta),Column(G),Upper Top(U.T.) section, Base(1),also uses the Direct Physical movement to displace to Row(8),Column(G),Top Center(T.C.) Platform, Base(1).

Folder 21 / # 8841 – Presents the Position BEFORE the Displacement (P.B.D.) of the chess pieces for Equation 15.

15. O.R. (I b(Kn (gamma prime) 3/ Kn (gamma prime) 6 - I b(Kn A2/ Kn A7) ;
             B.L.(0)   B.L.(0)   T.C.(1)   T.C.(1)
; II w(Kn (gamma prime) 3 / Kn (gamma prime) 6 - II w(Kn H4 / Kn H5)).
      B.R.(0)   B.R.(0)   B.C.(0)   B.C.(0)

Folder 21 / # 8842 – Displays the Position AFTER the Displacement (P.A.D) of the chess pieces for Equation 15.

15. O.R. (I b(Kn (gamma prime) 3 / Kn (gamma prime) 6 - I b(Kn A2 / Kn A7) ;
           B.L.(0)   B.L.(0)   T.C.(1)   T.C.(1)
; II w(Kn (gamma prime) 3 / Kn (gamma prime) 6 - I w(Kn H4 / Kn H5)).
    B.R.(0)   B.R.(0)   B.C.(0)   B.C.(0)

In Equation 15,part 1,Sections(A/B),for Section(A),Player I (first) Orange-Red color band Black Knight that previously positioned at Row(gamma prime),Column(3), *Bottom Left (B.L.) section, Base(0),uses the *Direct Abstract 4/2 squares movement to displace to Row(A),Column(2),*Top Center(T.C.) Platform, Base(1) AND for Section(B), Player I (second) Black Knight that previously positioned at Row(gamma prime),Column(6), *Bottom Left (B.L.) section, Base(0),also uses the *Direct Abstract 4/2 squares movement to displace to Row(A),Column(7),*Top Center(T.C.) Platform, Base(1).

In Equation 15,part 2,Section(C/D),for Section(C),Player II (first) Orange-Red color band White Knight that previously stationed at Row(gamma prime),Column(3), Bottom Right (B.R.) section, Base(0),uses the Direct Physical 4/2 squares movement to displace to Row(H),Column(4),Bottom Center(B.C.) Platform, Base(0) AND for Section(D), Player II (second) White Knight that previously stationed at Row (gamma prime),Column(6), Bottom Right(B.R.) section, Base(0),also uses the Direct Physical 4/2 squares movement to displace to Row(H),Column(5),Bottom Center(B.C.) Platform, Base(0).

Folder 21 / # 8843 – Depicts the Position BEFORE the Displacement (P.B.D.) of the chess pieces for Equation 16.

16. O.B. (I w(Kn (gamma) C / Kn (gamma) F - I w(Kn B1 / Kn G1) ;
            L.B.(0)   L.B.(0)   T.C.(1)   T.C.(1)
; II b(Kn (gamma) C / Kn (gamma) F   - II b(Kn 8D / Kn 8E)).

Folder 21 / # 8844 - Demonstrates the Position AFTER the Displacement (P.A.D.) of the chess pieces in Equation 16.

16. O.B. (I w(Kn (gamma) C / Kn (gamma) F - I w(Kn B1 / Kn G1) ;
              L.B.(0)   L.B.(0)   T.C.(1)   T.C.(1)
; II b(Kn (gamma) C / Kn (gamma) F - II b(Kn 8D / Kn 8E)).
    U.B.(0)   U.B.(0)   T.C.(1)   T.C.(1)

In Equation 16,part 1,Sections(A/B),Player I (first) Orange-Blue color band White Knight that previously positioned at Row(gamma),Column(C),*Lower Bottom(L.B.) section, Base(0),uses the *Direct Abstract 4/2 squares movement to displace to Row (B),Column(1),*Top Center(T.C.) Platform, Base(1) AND for Section(B),Player I (second) White Knight that previously positioned at Row(gamma),Column(F), *Lower Bottom (L.B.) section, Base(0),also uses the *Direct Abstract 4/2 squares movement to displace to Row(G),Column(1),*Top Center(T.C.) Platform, Base(1).

In Equation 16,part 2,Sections(C/D),for Section(C),Player II (first) Orange-Blue color band Black Knight that previously stationed at Row(gamma),Column(C), *Upper Bottom (U.B.) section, Base(0),uses the *Direct Abstract 4/2 squares movement to displace to Row(8),Column(D),*Top Center(T.C.) Platform, Base(1) AND for Section(D),Player II (second) Black Knight that previously stationed at Row(gamma),Column(F),*Upper Bottom (U.B.) section, Base(0),also uses the *Direct Abstract 4/2 squares movement to displace to Row(8),Column(E),*Top Center(T.C.) Platform, Base(1).

Folder 21 / # 8845 – Demonstrates the Position BEFORE the Displacement (P.B.D.) of the chess pieces for Equation 17A.

17A. R.Y. (I b(B (beta) C / Q (sigma prime) 5   -   I b(B (alpha) D /
             U.T.(1)   T.L.(1)   U.T.(1)

   / I b(Q (gamma prime) 5)   ;
             T.L.(1)

; II w(Kn H4 / Kn H5) - II w(Kn F5 / Kn F4)).
  T.C.(1)   T.C.(1)   T.C.(1)   T.C.(1)

Folder 21 / # 8846 - Unveils the Position AFTER the Displacement (P.A.D.) of the chess pieces in Equation 17A.

17A. R.Y. (I b(B (beta) C/ Q (sigma prime) 5 - I b(B (alpha) D) /
                    U.T.(1)   T.L.(1)   U.T.(1)
       / I b(Q (gamma prime) 5) ;
             T.L.(1)
; II w(Kn H4 / Kn H5) - II w(Kn F5 / Kn F4)).
   T.C.(1)   T.C.(1)   T.C.(1)   T.C.(1)

In Equation 17A,part 1,Sections(A/B),for Section(A),Player I Red-Yellow color band Black Bishop that previously positioned at Row(beta),Column(C),Upper Top(U.T.) section, Base (1),uses the Direct Physical diagonal movement to displace to Row (alpha),Column (D),Upper Top(U.T.) section, Base(1) AND for Section(B),Player I Black Queen that previously positioned at Row(sigma prime),Column(5),Top Left (T.L.) section, Base (1),also uses the Direct Physical single space movement to displace to Row(gamma prime), Column(5),Top Left(T.L.) section, Base(1).

In Equation 17A,part 2,Sections(C/D),for Section(C),Player II (first) Red-Yellow color band White Knight that previously stationed at Row(H),Column(4),Top Center(T.C.) Platform, Base(1),uses the Direct Physical 3/2 squares movement to displace to Row(F),Column(5),Top Center(T.C.) Platform, Base(1) AND for Section (D),Player II (second) White Knight that previously stationed at Row(H),Column (5),Top Center(T.C.) Platform, Base(1),also uses the Direct Physical 3/2 squares movement to displace to Row(F),Column(4),Top Center(T.C.) Platform, Base(1).

Folder 21 / # 8847 – Depicts the Position BEFORE the Displacement (P.B.D.) of the chess pieces for Equation 17B.

17B. R.Y. (I b(Q (gamma prime) 5 - Q (beta) C) ;   II w(Forfeits turn to play)).
        T.L.(1)   U.T.(1)

Folder 21 / # 8848 – Presents the Position AFTER the Displacement (P.A.D.) of the chess pieces for Equation 17B.

17B. R.Y.   (I b(Q (gamma prime) 5 - Q (beta) C) ; II w(Forfeits turn to play)).
                    T.L.(1)   U.T.(1)

In Equation 17B,part 1,Section(A),Player I Red-Yellow color band Black Queen that previously positioned at Row(gamma prime),Column(5),Top Left(T.L.) section, Base (1),uses the Direct Physical diagonal movement to displace to Row(beta),Column (C),Upper Top(U.T.) section, Base(1).

In Equation 17B,part 2,Section(C),Player II forfeits the turn to play ; Player II does not move any chess pieces.

Folder 21 / # 8849 – Illustrates the Position BEFORE the Displacement (P.B.D.) of the chess pieces for Equation 18A.

18A. O.B. (I w(Ki (sigma) E/Q (sigma) D - I w(Ki (gamma) D/Q (gamma) E) ;
                    L.B.(0)   L.B.(0)   L.T.(1)   L.T.(1)
; II b(Ki (sigma) E / Q (sigma) D) - II b(Ki (sigma) D/ Q (sigma) E)   ).
        U.B.(0)   U.B.(0)   U.B.(0)   U.B.(0)

Folder 21 / # 8852 - Unveils the Position AFTER the Displacement (P.A.D.) of the chess pieces for Equation 18A.

18A. O.B. (I w(Ki (sigma) E/Q (sigma) D - I w(Ki (gamma) D/Q (gamma) E) ;
         L.B.(0)   L.B.(0)   L.T.(1)   L.T.(1)
 ; II b(Ki (sigma) E / Q (sigma) D - II b(Ki (gamma) D / Q (sigma) E)).
     U.B.(0)   U.B.(0)   U.B.(0)   U.B.(0)

In Equation 18A,part 1,Sections(A/B),for Section(A),Player I Orange-Blue color band White King that previously positioned at Row(sigma),Column(E),*Lower Bottom(L.B.) section, Base(0),uses the *Direct Abstract single space diagonal movement to displace to Row(gamma),Column(D),*Lower Top(L.T.) section, Base (1) AND for Section(B), Player I White Queen that previously positioned at Row (sigma),Column(D),*Lower Bottom(L.B.) section, Base(0),also uses the *Direct Abstract single space diagonal movement to displace to Row(gamma),Column(E), *Lower Top(L.T.) section, Base(1).

In Equation 18A,part 2,Sections(C/D),for Section(C),Player II Orange-Blue color band Black King that previously stationed at Row(sigma),Column(E),Upper Bottom(U.B.) section, Base(0),uses the Direct Physical single space diagonal movement to displace to Row(gamma),Column(D),Upper Bottom(U.B.) section, Base(0) AND for Section (D),Player II Black Queen that previously stationed at Row(sigma),Column(D),Upper Bottom (U.B.) section, Base(0),uses the single space movement to displace to Row(sigma), Column(E),Upper Bottom(U.B.) section, Base(0).

Folder 21 / # 8853 – Reveals the Position BEFORE the Displacement (P.B.D.) of the chess pieces for
Equation 18B.

18B. O.B. (I w(Player I forfeits the turn to play) ;
  ; II b(Ki (gamma) D / Q (sigma) E - II b(Ki (gamma) C / Q (gamma) F)).
        U.B.(0)   U.B.(0)   U.B.(0)   U.B.(0)

Folder 21 / # 8854 – Examines the Position AFTER the Displacement (P.A.D.) of the chess pieces for Equation 18B.

18B.   O.B. (I w(Player I forfeits the turn to play) ;
   ; II b(Ki (gamma) D / Q (sigma) E - II b(Ki (gamma) C / Q (gamma) F)).
        U.B.(0)   U.B.(0)   U.B.(0)   U.B.(0)

In Equation 18B,part 1,Section(A),Player I forfeits the turn to play.

In Equation 18B,part 2,Sections(C/D),for Section(C),Player II Orange-Blue color band Black King that previously stationed at Row(gamma),Column(D),Upper Bottom(U.B.) section, Base(0),uses the Direct Physical single space movement to displace to Row (gamma),Column(C),Upper Bottom(U.B.) section, Base(0) AND for Section(D), Player II Black Queen that previously stationed at Row(sigma), Column (E),Upper Bottom(U.B.) section, Base(0),also uses the Direct Physical single space movement to displace to Row(gamma),Column(F),Upper Bottom(U.B.) section, Base(0).

Folder 21 / # 8855 – Explains the Position BEFORE the Displacement (P.B.D.) of the chess pieces for Equation 19.

19. O.R. (I b(Kn A2 / Kn A7) - I b(Kn (alpha) B / Kn (alpha) B)   ;
               T.C.(1)   T.C.(1)   L.B.(0)   U.T.(1)
 ; II w (B (gamma prime) 4 / B (gamma prime) 5) -
      B.R.(0)   B.R.(0)
  - II w(B (gamma)D / B (sigma) D)) .
        U.B.(0)   U.B.(0)

Folder 21 / # 8856 – Discloses the Position AFTER the Displacement (P.A.D.) of the chess pieces for Equation 19.

19. O.R. (I b(Kn A2 / Kn A7) - I b(Kn (alpha) B / Kn (alpha) B) ;
            T.C.(1)   T.C.(1)   L.B.(0)   U.T.(1)
; II w(B (gamma prime) 4 / B (gamma prime) 5 -
        B.R.(0)   B.R.(0)
  - II w(B (gamma) D / B (sigma) D)).
        U.B.(0)   U.B.(0)

In Equation 19,part 1,Sections(A/B),for Section(A),Player I (first) Orange-Red color band Black Knight that previously positioned at Row(A),Column(2),*Top Center (T.C.) Platform, Base(1),uses the *Direct Abstract 3/2 squares movement to displace to Row(alpha), Column(B),*Lower Bottom(L.B.) section, Base(0) AND for Section (B),Player I (second) Black Knight that previously positioned at Row(A),Column(7), Top Center(T.C.) Platform, Base(1),uses the Direct Physical 3/2 squares movement to displace to Row(alpha),Column(B),Upper Top(U.T.) section, Base(1).

In Equation 19,part 2,Sections(C/D),for Section(C),Player II (first) Orange-Red color band White Bishop that previously stationed at Row(gamma prime), Column (4),Bottom Right(B.R.) section, Base(0),uses the Direct Physical diagonal movement to displace to Row(gamma),Column(D),Upper Bottom(U.B.) section, Base(0) AND for Section (D),Player II (second) White Bishop that previously stationed at Row (gamma prime),Column(5), Bottom Right(B.R.) section, Base(0),also uses the Direct Physical diagonal movement to displace to Row(sigma),Column(D),Upper Bottom(U.B.) section, Base(0).

Folder 21 / # 8857 – Discloses the Position BEFORE the Displacement (P.B.D.) of the chess pieces for Equation 20A.

20A.   R.P.   (I w(Ki (sigma) E /   Q (sigma) D   ) -
                         L.T.(1)   L.T.(1)
   -   I w(Ki (gamma) D / Q (gamma) E)   ;
                   L.B.(0)   L.B.(0)
; II b(Player II forfeits the turn to play)   ).

Folder 21 / # 8858 – Reveals the Position AFTER the Displacement (P.A.D.) of the chess pieces for Equation 20A.

20A. R.P. (I w(Ki (sigma) E/Q (sigma) D) - I w(Ki (gamma) D/Q (gamma) E) ;

$\qquad$ L.T.(1) $\qquad$ L.T.(1) $\qquad$ L.B.(0) $\qquad$ L.B.(0)

 ; II b(Player II forfeits the turn to play)   ).

In Equation 20A, part 1, Sections(A/B), for Section(A), Player I Red-Purple color band White King that previously positioned at Row(sigma), Column(E), Lower Top(L.T.) section, Base (1), uses the Direct Abstract single space diagonal movement to displace to Row (gamma), Column(D), Lower Bottom(L.B.) section, Base(0) AND for Section(B), Player I White Queen that previously positioned at Row(sigma), Column (D), Lower Top(L.T.) section, Base(1), also uses the Direct Abstract single space diagonal movement to displace to Row(gamma), Column(E), Lower Bottom(L.B.) section, Base(0).

In Equation 20A, part 2, Section(A), Player II forfeits the turn to play.

Folder 21 / # 8859 – Presents the Position BEFORE the Displacement (P.B.D.) of the chess pieces for Equation 20B.

20B.   R.Y.   (I b(Ki (sigma prime) 4 – Ki (gamma prime) 4   ) ;
                     T.L.(1)   T.L.(1)
  ; II w(Player II forfeits the turn to play)

Folder 21 / # 8860 – Depicts the Position AFTER the Displacement (P.A.D.) of the chess pieces for Equation 20B.

20B.   R.Y. (I b(Ki (sigma prime) 4 - Ki (gamma prime) 4) ;
             T.L.(1)   T.L.(1)
; II w(Player II forfeits the turn to play)).

In Equation 20B, part 1, Player I Red-Yellow color band Black King that previously positioned at Row(sigma prime), Column(4), Top Left(T.L.) section, Base(1), uses the Direct Physical single space movement to displace to Row(gamma prime), Column (4), Top Left(T.L.) section, Base(1).

In Equation 20B, part 2, Player II forfeits the turn to play ; Player II does not move any of the chess pieces.

Folder 21 / # 8861 – Illustrates the Position BEFORE the Displacement (P.B.D.) of the chess pieces for Equation 20C.

20C.   R.P. (I w(Player I forfeits the turn to play) ;
     ; II b(B (gamma) D / B (gamma) E   )   -
         U.T.(1)   U.T.(1)
    - II b(B (sigma prime) 4 / B (gamma prime) 5)).
         T.L.(1)   B.R.(0)

Folder 21 / # 8862 – Discloses the Position AFTER the Displacement (P.A.D.) of the chess pieces for Equation 20C.

20C.   R.P.   (I w (Player I forfeits the turn to play)   ;

; II b(B (gamma) D / B (gamma) E) -
          U.T.(1)   U.T.(1)
  - II b(B (sigma prime) 4 / B (gamma prime) 5)).
          T.L.(1)   B.R.(0)

In Equation 20C,part 1,Player I forfeits the turn to play ; Player I does not move any chess pieces.

In Equation 20C,part 2,Sections(C/D),for Section(C),Player II (first) Red-Purple color band Black Bishop that previously stationed at Row(gamma),Column (D), Upper Top(U.T.) section, Base(1),uses the Direct Physical diagonal movement to displace to Row (sigma prime),Column(4),Top Left(T.L.) section, Base(1) AND for Section(D),Player II (second) Black Bishop that previously stationed at Row (gamma),Column(E),*Upper Top (U.T.) section, Base(1),uses the *Direct Abstract diagonal movement to displace to Row (gamma prime),Column(5),*Bottom Right (B.R.) section, Base(0).

Folder 21 / # 8863 – Displays the Position BEFORE the Displacement (P.B.D.) of the chess pieces for Equation 21A.

21A. R.P. (I w(B (beta) E / B (beta) D) - I w(B (beta) E)   X
                    L.B.(0)   L.B.(0)   L.B.(0)
     X   II b(B (gamma prime) 5) /   I w(B (beta) D - B (alpha) C)   ;
                    B.R.(0)   L.B.(0)   L.B.(0)
;   II b(B (sigma prime) 4   X   I w(C (beta) B)   ).
          T.L.(1)   L.T.(1)

Folder 21 / # 8864 – Exhibits the Position AFTER the Displacement (P.A.D.) of the chess pieces for Equation 21A.

21A. R.P. (I w(B (beta) E / B (beta) D) - I w(B (beta) E)   X
             L.B.(0)   L.B.(0)   L.B.(0)
    X   II b(B (gamma prime) 5 /   I w(B (beta) D - B (alpha) C)   ;
             B.R.(0)   L.B.(0)   L.B.(0)
; II b(B (sigma prime) 4   X   I w(C (beta) B   )).
    T.L.(1)   L.T.(1)

In Equation 21A,part 1,Sections (A/B),for Section(A),Player I (first) Red-Purple color band White Bishop that previously positioned at Row(beta),Column(E),Lower Bottom(L.B.) section, Base(0),uses the Direct Physical diagonal attack movement to capture Player II Black Bishop that stations at Row(gamma prime),Column(5), Bottom Right(B.R.) section, Base(0) AND for Section(B),Player I (second) White Bishop that previously positioned at Row(beta),Column(D),Lower Bottom(L.B.) section, Base(0),uses the Direct Physical single space diagonal movement to displace to Row(alpha),Column(C), Lower Bottom(L.B.) section, Base(0).

In Equation 21A,part 2,Section(C),for Section(C),Player II Red-Purple color band Black Bishop that previously stationed at Row(sigma prime),Column(4),Top Left (T.L.) section, Base(1),uses the Direct Physical diagonal attack movement to capture Player I White Castle that positions at Row(beta),Column(B),Lower Top (L.T.) section, Base(1).

Folder 21 / # 8865 – Presents the Position BEFORE the Displacement (P.B.D.) of the chess pieces for Equation 21B.

21B. R.P. (I w(P (alpha) E / Q (gamma) E   - I w(P 1E / Q (alpha) E) ;
                    L.T.(1)   L.B.(0)   T.C.(1)   T.C.(1)
; II b(Kn (gamma) F - Kn (alpha) G)).
      U.T.(1)   U.T.(1)

Folder 21 / # 8866 – Unveils the Position AFTER the Displacement (P.A.D.) of the chess pieces for Equation 21B.

21B. R.P. (I w(P (alpha) E / Q (gamma) E) - I w(P 1E / Q (alpha) E) ;
             L.T.(1)   L.B.(0)   T.C.(1)   T.C.(1)
; II b(Kn (gamma) F - Kn (alpha) G)).
    U.T.(1)   U.T.(1)

In Equation 21B,part 1,Section(A/B),for Section(A),Player I Red-Purple color band White Pawn that previously positioned at Row(alpha),Column(E),Lower Top(L.T.) section, Base (1),uses the Direct Physical single space <u>vertical</u> (Chess Set # 3,the Third Group of letters having an (A-A) initial position set-up) movement to displace to Row(1), Column(E),Top Center(T.C.) Platform, Base(1) AND for Section(B), Player I White Queen that previously positioned at Row(gamma),Column(E),*Lower Bottom(L.B.) section, Base (0),uses the *Direct Abstract movement to displace to Row(alpha),Column(E), *Top Center(T.C.) Platform, Base(1).

In Equation 21B,part 2,Player II Red-Purple color band Black Knight that previously stationed at Row(gamma),Column(F),Upper Top(U.T.) section, Base(1),uses the Direct Physical 3/2 squares movement to displace to Row(alpha),Column(G),Upper Top(U.T.) section, Base(1).

Folder 21 / # 8867 – Unveils the Position BEFORE the Displacement (P.B.D.) of the chess pieces for Equation 21C.

21C. R.P. (I w(Q (alpha) E - Q (gamma prime) 6) ;
               L.T.(1)   B.R.(0)
; II b(Player II forfeits the turn to play)).

Folder 21 / # 8868 – Reveals the Position AFTER the Displacement (P.A.D.) of the chess pieces for Equation 21C.

21C. R.P. (I w(Q (alpha) E - Q (gamma prime) 6)   ;
              L.T.(1)   B.R.(0)
 ; II b(Player II forfeits the turn to play)   ).

In Equation 21C,part 1,Player I Red-Purple color band White Queen that previously positioned at Row(alpha),Column(E),*Lower Top(L.T.) section, Base(1),uses the *Direct Abstract diagonal movement to displace to Row(gamma prime),Column(6), *Bottom Right (B.R.) section, Base(0).

Folder 21 - # 8869 – Examines the Position BEFORE the Capture (P.B.C.) of Player II Red-Purple color band Black King that stations at Row(sigma),Column(E),Upper Top(U.T.) section, Base(1) by Player I White Queen that positions at Row(gamma prime),Column(6),Bottom Right(B.R.) section, Base(0) for Equation 22.   [END] 1.

22. R.P. (I w(Q (gamma prime) 6   )   X   II b(Ki (sigma) E)   ;   ………….……
                     B.R.(0)   U.T.(1)   [END] 1.

Folder 21/ # 8870 - Explains the Position AFTER the Capture (P.A.C.) of Player II Red-Purple color band Black King that previously stationed at Row(sigma), Column (E),Upper Top(U.T.) section, Base(1) by Player Red-Purple color band White Queen that previously positioned at Row(gamma prime),Column(6),Bottom Right(B.R.) section, Base(0) for Equation 22.

22.   R.P.   (I w(Q (gamma prime) 6   X   II b(Ki (sigma) E) ; …………………..
              B.R.(0)   U.T.(1)   [END] 1.

In Equation 22,part 1,Player I Red-Purple color band White Queen that previously positioned at Row(gamma prime),Column(6),Bottom Right(B.R.) section, Base(0),uses the Direct Abstract diagonal Stealth (silent) [CHECKMATE] attack to capture Player II Red-Purple color band Black King that previously stationed at Row(sigma),Column(E),Upper Top(U.T.) section, Base(1).   Player I wins the Red-Purple color band set. [END] 1.   The match continues with the Orange-Blue, Orange-Red and Red-Yellow color band sets.

Folder 21 / # 8871 – Explains the Position BEFORE the Displacement (P.B.D.) of the chess pieces for Equation 23.

23. R.Y. (I b(Kn (gamma prime) 3/Kn (gamma prime) 6 - I b(Kn A4/ Kn A5) ;

              T.L.(1)   T.L.(1)   B.C.(0)   B.C.(0)

 ; II w(Kn F4 / Kn F5)   X I b(P D3 / P D4)).

  T.C.(1)   T.C.(1)   T.C.(1)   T.C.(1)

Folder 21 / # 8872 - Presents the Position AFTER the Displacement (P.A.D.) of the chess pieces for Equation 23.

23. R.Y. (I b(Kn (gamma prime) 3/ Kn (gamma prime) 6 - I b(Kn A4/ Kn A5) ;
        T.L.(1)   T.L.(1)   B.C.(0)   B.C.(0)
 ; II w(Kn F4 / Kn F5)   X   I b(P D3 / P D4)).
  T.C.(1)   T.C.(1)   T.C.(1)   T.C.(1)

In Equation 23,part 1,Sections(A/B),for Section(A),Player I (first) Red-Yellow color band Black Knight that previously positioned at Row(gamma prime),Column(3),Top Left(T.L.) section, Base(1),uses the Direct Abstract 4/2 squares movement to displace to Row(A),Column(4),Bottom Center(B.C.) Platform, Base(0) AND for Section(B),Player I (second) Black Knight that previously positioned at Row(gamma prime),Column(6),Top Left(T.L.) section, Base(1),also uses the Direct Abstract 4/2 squares movement to displace to Row(A),Column(5),Bottom Center(B.C.) Platform, Base(0).

Equation 23,part 2,Sections(C/D) is a Double Captivity equation. In Equation 23, part 2,Sections(C/D),for Section(C),Player II (first) Red-Yellow color band White Knight that previously stationed at Row(F),Column(4),Top Center(T.C.) Platform, Base(1),uses the Direct Physical 3/2 squares attack movement to capture Player I (first) Black Pawn that previously positioned at Row(D),Column(3),Top Center(T.C.) Platform, Base(1) AND for Section(D),Player II (second) White Knight that previously stationed at Row(F),Column(5),Top Center(T.C.) Platform, Base(1),also uses the Direct Physical 3/2 squares attack movement to capture Player I (second) Black Pawn that previously positioned at Row(D),Column(4),Top Center(T.C.) Platform, Base(1).

Folder 21 / # 8873 – Reveals the Position BEFORE the Displacement (P.B.D.) of the chess pieces for Equation 24.

24. O.R.   (I b(C (beta prime) 2 / P (alpha prime) 1 - I b(C B2 / P B1   ) ;
            B.L.(0)   B.L.(0)   B.C.(0)   B.C.(0)
; II w(Kn H4 / Kn H5) - II w(Kn E5 / Kn E 4)).
    B.C.(0)   B.C.(0)   B.C.(0)   B.C.(0)

Folder 21 / # 8874 - Explains the Position AFTER the Displacement (P.A.D.) of the chess pieces for Equation 24.

24. O.R.   (I b(C (beta prime) 2 / P (alpha prime) 1 - I b(C B2/ P B1) ;
              B.L.(0)   B.L.(0)   B.C.(0)   B.C.(0)
 ; II w(Kn H4 / Kn H5) - II w(Kn E5 / Kn E4)).
   B.C.(0)   B.C.(0)   B.C.(0)   B.C.(0)

In Equation 24,part 1,Sections(A/B),for Section(A),Player I Orange-Red color band Black Castle that previously positioned at Row(beta prime),Column(2),Bottom Left (B.L.) section, Base(0),uses the Direct Physical movement to displace to Row (B), Column(2),Bottom Center(B.C.) Platform, Base(0) AND for Section (B),Player I Black Pawn that previously positioned at Row(alpha prime),Column(1),Bottom Left (B.L.) section, Base(0),also uses the Direct Physical movement to displace to Row (B),Column(1),Bottom Center(B.C.) Platform, Base(0).

In Equation 24,part 2,Sections(C/D),for Section(C),Player II (first) Orange-Red color band White Knight that previously stationed at Row(H),Column(4),Bottom Center(B.C.) Platform, Base(0),uses the Direct Physical 4/2 squares movement to displace to Row(E),Column(5),Bottom Center(B.C.) Platform, Base(0) AND for Section(D),Player II (second) White Knight that previously stationed at Row(H), Column(5),Bottom Center(B.C.) Platform, Base(0),also uses the Direct Physical 4/2 squares movement to displace to Row(E),Column(4),Bottom Center(B.C.) Platform, Base(0).

Folder 21 / # 8875 – Demonstrates the Position BEFORE the Displacement (P.B.D.) of the chess pieces for Equation 25A.

25A.   O.R.   (I b(B (gamma prime) 5)   X   II w(B (gamma) D)   /
                B.L.(0)   U.B.(0)
  /   I b(Kn (alpha) B - Kn C3)   ;
        L.B.(0)   B.C.(0)
; II w(Kn E4)   X   I b(Kn   C3)   /   II w(Kn E5 - Kn C6)   ).
   B.C.(0)   B.C.(0)   B.C.(0)   B.C.(0)

Folder 21 / # 8876 – Presents the Position AFTER the Displacement (P.A.D.) for the chess pieces for Equation 25A.

25A. O.R. (I b(B (gamma prime) 5 X II w(B (gamma) D   /
                    B.L.(0)   U.B.(0)
    / I b(Kn (alpha) B - Kn C3) ;
             L.B.(0)   B.C.(0)
; II w(Kn E4) X I b(Kn C3) / II w(Kn E 5 - Kn C6)).
    B.C.(0)   B.C.(0)   B.C.(0)   B.C.(0)

In Equation 25A,part 1,Sections(A/B),for Section(A),Player I Orange-Red color band Black Bishop that previously positioned at Row(gamma prime),Column(5),Bottom Left(B.L.) section, Base(0),uses the Direct Physical diagonal attack movement to capture Player II White Bishop that previously stationed at Row(gamma),Column (D),Upper Bottom(U.B.) section, Base(0) AND for Section(B),Player I Orange-Red color band Black Knight that previously positioned at Row(alpha),Column(B),Lower Bottom(L.B.) section, Base(0),uses the Direct Physical 4/2 squares movement to displace to Row(C),Column(3),Bottom Center(B.C.) Platform, Base(0).

In Equation 25A,part 2,Sections(C/D),for Section(C),Player II (first) Orange-Red color band White Knight that previously stationed at Row(E),Column(4),Bottom Center(B.C.) Platform, Base(0),uses the Direct Physical 3/2 squares attack movement to capture Player I Black Knight that previously positioned at Row(C), Column(3),Bottom Center(B.C.) Platform, Base(0).

LOGIC: Player II (first) White Knight now poises an imminent Direct Abstract 4/2 squares THREAT to Player I Black Knight that positions at Row(alpha),Column(B), Upper Top(U.T.) section, Base(1).

In Equation 25A,part 2,Section(D),Player II (second) White Knight that previously stationed at Row(E),Column(5),Bottom Center(B.C.) Platform, Base(0),uses the Direct Physical 3/2 squares movement to displace to Row(C),Column(6),Bottom Center(B.C.) Platform, Base(0).

Folder 21 /# 8877 - Examines the Position BEFORE the Displacement (P.B.D.) of the chess pieces for Equation 25B.

25B.   O.R.   (I b(B (gamma) D / B (gamma prime) 4 -
                    U.B.(0)   B.L.(0)
    - I b(B (sigma) E / B (sigma) E)   ;
            U.T.(1)   L.T.(1)
; II w(P F8/ P F1) - II w(P C8 / P C1)).
  B.C.(0)   B.C.(0)   T.C.(1)   T.C.(1)

Folder 21 / # 8878 - Exhibits the Position AFTER the Displacement (P.A.D.) of the chess pieces for Equation 25B.

25B. O.R. (I b(B (gamma) D / B (gamma prime) 4   -
                    U.B.(0)   B.L.(0)
  - I b(B (sigma) E / B (sigma) E) ;
          U.T.(1)   L.T.(1)
 ; II w(P F8 / P F1) - II w(P C8 / P C 1)) .
   B.C.(0)   B.C.(0)   T.C.(1)   T.C.(1)

In Equation 25B,part 1,Sections(A/B),for Section(A),Player I (first) Orange-Red color band Black Bishop that previously positioned at Row(gamma),Column(D), Upper Bottom(U.B.) section, Base(0),uses the Direct Abstract single space diagonal movement to displace to Row(sigma),Column(E),Upper Top(U.T.) section, Base(1) AND for Section(B),Player I (second) Black Bishop that previously positioned at Row(gamma prime),Column(4),Bottom Left(B.L.) section, Base(0),also uses the Direct Abstract single space diagonal movement to displace to Row(sigma),Column (E),Lower Top(L.T.) section, Base(1).

In Equation 25B,part 2,Sections(C/D),for Section(C),Player II (first) Orange-Red color band White Pawn that previously stationed at Row(F),Column(8),*Bottom Center(B.C.) Platform, Base(0),uses the *Direct Abstract <u>horizontal</u> (Chess Set # 2, the Second Group of letters having a (G-G) initial position set-up) movement (unto the second immediate available vacant square) to displace to Row(C),Column(8), *Top Center(T.C) Platform, Base(1) AND for Section(D),Player II (second) White Pawn that previously stationed at Row(F),Column(1),*Bottom Center(B.C.) Platform, Base(0),also uses the *Direct Abstract movement to displace to Row(C),Column(1),*Top Center(T.C.) Platform, Base(1).

LOGIC: In Equation 25B,part 2,Section(C),Player II (first) Orange-Red color band White Pawn that stations at Row(C),Column(8),Top Center(T.C.) Platform, Base(1), now poises a Direct Abstract single space diagonal THREAT to Player I Black Knight that positions at Row(alpha),Column(B),Upper Top(U.T.) section, Base(1).

LOGIC: In Equation 25B,part 2,Section(D),Player II (second) Orange-Red color band White Pawn that stations at Row(C),Column(1),Top Center(T.C.) Platform, Base(1),now poises an imminent Direct Abstract single space diagonal THREAT to Player I Black Castle that positions at Row(B),Column(2),Bottom Center(B.C.) Platform, Base(0).

Folder 21 / # 8879 – Exhibits the Position BEFORE the Displacement (P.B.D.) of the chess pieces for Equation 25C.

25C. O.R. (I b(P C2 - P D2)/ I b(B (sigma) E)   X   II w(C (beta prime) 7) ;
       T.C.(1)   T.C.(1)   U.T.(1)   B.R.(0)
; II w(P C1 / C (beta prime) 2)   X   I b(C B2 / B (beta prime) 7)   ).
    T.C.(1)   B.R.(0)   B.C.(0)   B.R.(0)

Folder 21 / # 8880 - Examines the Position AFTER the Displacement (P.A.D.) of the chess pieces for Equation 25C.

25C. O.R. (I b(P C2 - P D2)/I b(B (sigma) E) X II w (C (beta prime) 7) ;
        T.C.(1)   T.C.(1)   U.T.(1)   B.R.(0)
; II w(P C1 / C (beta prime) 2) X I b(C B2 / B (beta prime) 7)).
 T.C.(1)   B.R.(0)   B.C.(0)   B.R.(0)

In Equation 25C,part 1,Sections(A/B),for Section(A),Player I Orange-Red color band Black Pawn that previously positioned at Row(C),Column(2),Top Center(T.C.) Platform, Base(1),uses the Direct Physical single space <u>horizontal</u> (Chess Set # 2, the Second Group of letters having a (G-G) initial position configuration) movement to displace to Row(D),Column(2),Top Center(T.C.) Platform, Base(1) AND for Section (B),Player I Black Bishop that previously positioned at Row(sigma),Column (E), Upper Top(U.T.) section, Base(1),uses the Direct Abstract diagonal attack movement to capture Player II White Castle that previously stationed at Row(beta prime), Column(7),Bottom Right(B.R.) section, Base(0)

In Equation 25C,part 2,Sections(C/D),for Section(C),Player II Orange-Red color band White Pawn that previously stationed at Row(C),Column(1),Top Center(T.C.) Platform, Base(1),uses the Direct Abstract single space diagonal attack movement to capture Player I Black Castle that previously positioned at Row(B),Column(2), Bottom Center(B.C.) Platform, Base(0) AND for Section(D),Player II White Castle that previously stationed at Row(beta prime),Column(2),Bottom Right(B.R.) section, Base(0),uses the Direct Physical attack movement to capture Player I Black Bishop that previously positioned at Row(beta prime),Column(7),Bottom Right(B.R.) section, Base(0).

LOGIC: In Equation 25C, part 2, Section(D), the movement of Player II White Castle at Row(beta prime), Column(2), Bottom Right(B.R.) section, Base(0) to capture Player I Black Bishop at Row(beta prime), Column(7), Bottom Right(B.R.) section, Base(0), leaves Player II Orange-Red color band White King open and vulnerable to Player I Black Bishop Stealth (silent) [CHECKMATE] capture attack from the position of Row(sigma), Column(E), Lower Top(L.T.) section, Base(1).

Folder 21 / # 8881 – Discloses the Position BEFORE the [CHECKMATE] Capture of Player II Orange-Red color band White King that stations at Row(sigma prime), Column(4), Bottom Right(B.R.) section, Base(0), by Player I Black Bishop that positions at Row(sigma), Column(E), Lower Top(L.T.) section, Base(1) for Equation 26.

26. O.R. (I b(B (sigma) E)   X II w(Ki (sigma prime) 4 ; ....
               L.T.(1)   B.R.(0)   [END] 2.

Folder 21 / # 8882 – Reveals the Position AFTER the [CHECKMATE] Capture of Player II Orange-Red color band White King that previously stationed at Row(sigma prime),Column(4),Bottom Right(B.R.) section, Base(0),by Player I Black Bishop that previously positioned at Row(sigma),Column(E),Lower Top(L.T.) section, Base(1) for Equation 26.

Player I wins the Orange-Red color band set. [END] 2. The match continues with the Orange-Blue and Red-Yellow color band sets.

26. O.R. (I b(B (sigma) E)   X   II w(Ki (sigma prime) 4) ; ……………………
              L.T.(1)   B.R.(0)   [END] 2.

In Equation 26,part 1,Player I Orange-Red color band Black Bishop that previously positioned at Row(sigma),Column(E),Lower Top(L.T.) section, Base(1),uses the Direct Abstract diagonal Stealth (silent) [CHECKMATE] attack to capture Player II White King that previously stationed at Row(sigma prime),Column(4),Bottom Right(B.R.) section, Base(0).   Player I wins the Orange-Red color band set. [END] 2.

Folder 21 / # 8884 – Shows the Position BEFORE the Displacement (P.B.D.) of the chess pieces for Equation 27A.

27A. R.Y. (I b(B (alpha) D/ Q (beta) C) -   I b(B (gamma) F/Q (sigma) E) ;
                    U.T.(1)   U.T.(1)   U.T.(1)   U.B.(0)
; II w(Kn D3 / Kn D4) X I b(Kn A4 / Kn A5)   ).
    T.C.(1)   T.C.(1)   B.C.(0)   B.C.(0)

Folder 21 / # 8885 - Represents the Position AFTER the Displacement (P.A.D.) of the chess pieces for Equation 27A.

27A. R.Y. (I b(B (alpha) D/Q (beta) C) - I b(B (gamma) F/Q (sigma) E) ;
             U.T.(1)   U.T.(1)   U.T.(1)   U.B.(0)
; II w(Kn D3 / Kn D4) X I b(Kn A4/ Kn A5)).
 T.C.(1)   T.C.(1)   B.C.(0)   B.C.(0)

In Equation 27A,part 1,Sections(A/B),for Section(A),Player I Red-Yellow color band Black Bishop that previously positioned at Row(alpha),Column(D),Upper Top(U.T.) section, Base(1),uses the Direct Physical diagonal movement to displace to Row (gamma),Column(F),Upper Top(U.T.) section, Base(1) AND for Section(B),Player I Black Queen that previously positioned at Row(beta),Column(C),*Upper Top(U.T.) section, Base(1),uses the *Direct Abstract diagonal movement to displace to Row (sigma),Column(E),*Upper Bottom(U.B.) section, Base(0).

In Equation 27A,part 2,Sections(C/D),for Section(C),Player II (first) Red-Yellow color band White Knight that previously stationed at Row(D),Column(3),*Top Center(T.C.) Platform, Base(1),uses the *Direct Abstract 4/2 squares attack movement to capture Player I (first) Black Knight that previously positioned at Row (A),Column (4),*Bottom Center(B.C.) Platform, Base(0) AND for Section(D),Player II (second) White Knight that previously stationed at Row(D),Column(4),*Top Center(T.C.) Platform, Base(1),also uses the *Direct Abstract 4/2 squares attack movement to capture Player I (second) Black Knight that previously positioned at Row(A),Column (5),*Bottom Center(B.C.) Platform, Base(0). Thus Equation 27A, part 2 is a DOUBLE CAPTIVITY Equation.

Folder 21 / # 8886 – Presents the Position BEFORE the Displacement (P.B.D.) of the chess pieces for Equation 27B. Player II Red-Yellow color band White Knight that stations at Row(A),Column(5),Bottom Center(B.C.) Platform, Base(0),uses the Direct Abstract 4/2 squares Stealth (silent) [CHECKMATE] attack movement to capture Player I Red-Yellow color band Black King that positions at Row(gamma prime),Column(4),Top Left(T.L.) section, Base(1).

27B. R.Y. (I b(B (beta) D / P B2) - I b(B (beta prime) 5 / P C2   ) ;
                U.T.(1)   T.C.(1)   T.L.(1)   T.C.(1)
; II w(Kn A5 / Kn A4)   X   I b(Ki (gamma prime) 4 / Kn (beta prime) 5   ).
    B.C.(0)   B.C.(0)   T.L.(1)   T.L.(1)
                        [END] 3.

Folder 21 / # 8887 – Explains the Position AFTER the [CHECKMATE] capture of Player I Red-Yellow color band Black King that previously positioned at Row (gamma prime),Column(4),Top Left(T.L.) section, Base(1) by Player II White Knight that previously stationed at Row(A),Column(5),Bottom Center(B.C.) Platform, Base(0) for Equation 27B.

27B.   R.Y. (I b(B (beta) D / P B2) - I b(B (beta prime) 5 / P C2) ;
                    U.T.(1)   T.C.(1)   T.L.(1)   T.C.(1)
; II w(Kn A5/ Kn A4)   X   I b(Ki (gamma prime) 4/ Kn (beta prime) 5)).
  B.C.(0)   B.C.(0)   T.L.(1)   T.L.(1)
                              [END] 3.

In Equation 27B,part 1,Sections(A/B),for Section(A),Player I Red-Yellow color band Black Bishop that previously positioned at Row(beta),Column(D),Upper Top(U.T.) section, Base(1),uses the Direct Physical diagonal movement to displace to Row(beta prime),Column(5),Top Left(T.L.) section, Base(1) AND for Section(B),Player I Black Pawn that previously positioned at Row(B),Column(2),Top Center(T.C.) Platform, Base(1),also uses the Direct Physical single space <u>horizontal</u> (Chess Set # 4,the Fourth Group of letters having an (A-A) initial position set-up) movement to displace to Row(C),Column(2),Top Center(T.C.) Platform, Base(1).

In Equation 27B,part 2,Sections(C/D),for Section(C),Player II (first) Red-Yellow color band White Knight that previously stationed at Row(A),Column(5),Bottom Center(B.C.) Platform, Base(0),uses the Direct

Abstract 4/2 squares attack movement to capture Player I Red-Yellow color band Black King that previously positioned at Row(gamma prime),Column(4),Top Left(T.L.) section, Base(1)

[END] 3. Player II wins the Red-Yellow color band set. The match continues with the Orange-Blue color band set.

For Section(D),Player II (second) White Knight that previously stationed at Row(A),Column(4),Bottom Center(B.C.) Platform, Base(0),also uses the Direct Abstract 3/2 squares attack movement to capture Player I Black Knight that previously positioned at Row(beta prime),Column(5),Top Left(T.L.) section, Base(1).

Folder 21 / # 8888 – Demonstrates the Position BEFORE the Displacement (P.B.D.) of the chess pieces for Equation 28.

28. O.B. (I w(Kn G1 / P (alpha) D   -   I w(Kn H3 / P 2D) ;
　　　　　　　T.C.(1)　　　　L.B.(0)　　　　T.C.(1)　　　　B.C.(0)
; II b(Kn 8D / Kn 8E) - II b(Kn 6C / Kn 7H)   ).
　T.C.(1)　　　T.C.(1)　　　T.C.(1)　　　　T.C.(1)

Folder 21 / # 8889 – Exhibits the Position AFTER the Displacement (P.A.D.) of the chess pieces for Equation 28.

28. O.B. (I w(Kn G1 / P (alpha) D) - I w(Kn H3/ P 2D)   ;
          T.C.(1)   L.B.(0)   T.C.(1)   B.C.(0)
; II b(Kn 8D / Kn 8E) - II b(Kn 6C / Kn 7H)).
  T.C.(1)   T.C.(1)   T.C.(1)   T.C.(1)

In Equation 28,part 1,Sections(A/B),for Section(A),Player I Orange-Blue color band White Knight that previously positioned at Row(G),Column(1),Top Center(T.C.) Platform, Base(1),uses the Direct Physical 3/2 squares movement to displace to Row (H),Column(3),Top Center(T.C.) Platform, Base(1) AND for Section(B),Player I White Pawn that previously positioned at Row(alpha),Column(D),Lower Bottom (L.B.) section, Base(0),uses the two spaces Direct Physical <u>vertical</u> (Chess Set # 1,the First Group of letters having a (G-G) initial position configuration) movement to displace to Row(2),Column(D),Bottom Center(B.C.) Platform, Base(0).

In Equation 28,part 2,Sections(C/D),for Section(C),Player II (first) Orange-Blue color band Black Knight that previously stationed at Row(8),Column(D),Top Center(T.C.) Platform, Base(1),uses the Direct Physical 3/2 squares movement to displace to Row(6),Column(C),Top Center(T.C.) Platform, Base(1) AND for Section(D),Player II (second) Black Knight that previously stationed at Row(8), Column(E),Top Center(T.C.) Platform, Base(1),uses the Direct Physical 4/2 squares movement to displace to Row(7),Column(H),Top Center(T.C.) Platform, Base(1).

Folder 21 / # 8890 - Demonstrates the Position BEFORE the Displacement (P.B.D.) of the chess pieces for Equation 29.

29. O.B. (I w(Q (gamma) E / Kn 1B) - I w(Q (gamma) F / Kn 4A) ;
              L.T.(1)   T.C.(1)   L.B.(0)   T.C.(1)
; II b(P (alpha) B / P (alpha) E - II b(P 7B / P 7E)).
    U.B.(0)   U.B.(0)   B.C.(0)   B.C.(0)

Folder 21 / # 8891 – Explains the Position AFTER the Displacement (P.A.D.) of the chess pieces for Equation 29.

29. O.B. (I w(Q (gamma) E / Kn 1B) - I w(Q (gamma) F / Kn 4A) ;
           L.T.(1)   T.C.(1)   L.B.(0)   T.C.(1)
; II b(P (alpha) B / P (alpha) E) - II b(P 7B / P 7E)).
  U.B.(0)   U.B.(0)   B.C.(0)   B.C.(0)

In Equation 29,part 1,Sections(A/B),for Section(A),Player I Orange-Blue color band White Queen that previously positioned at Row(gamma),Column(E),Lower Top (L.T.) section, Base(1),uses the Direct Abstract single space diagonal movement to displace to Row(gamma),Column(F),Lower Bottom(L.B.) section, Base(0) AND for Section(B),Player I White Knight that previously positioned at Row(1),Column(B), Top Center(T.C.) Platform, Base(1),uses the Direct Physical 4/2 squares movement to displace to Row(4),Column(A),Top Center(T.C.) Platform, Base(1).

In Equation 29,part 2,Sections(C/D),for Section(C),Player II (first) Orange-Blue color band Black Pawn that previously stationed at Row(alpha),Column(B),Upper Bottom(U.B.) section, Base(0),uses the Direct Physical two spaces <u>vertical</u> (Chess Set # 1,the First Group of letters having a (G-G) initial position set-up) movement (unto the second immediate available vacant square) to displace to Row(7),Column (B),Bottom Center(B.C.) Platform, Base(0) AND for Section(D),Player II (second) Black Pawn that previously stationed at Row(alpha),Column(E),Upper Bottom(U.B.) section, Base(0),also uses the Direct Physical two spaces movement to displace to Row(7),Column(E),Bottom Center(B.C.) Platform, Base(0).

Folder 21 / # 8892 – Illustrates the Position BEFORE the Displacement (P.B.D.) of the chess pieces for Equation 30.

30. O.B.   (I w(B (alpha) B/ Kn 3H) - I w(B (beta) C/ Kn (alpha prime) 5) ;
               L.T.(1)   T.C.(1)   L.T.(1)   B.R.(0)
; II b(Kn 7H)   X   I w(Kn (alpha prime) 5) / II b(P 7B - P 5B)).
     T.C.(1)   B.R.(0)   B.C.(0)   B.C.(0)

Folder 21 / # 8893 - Illustrates the Position AFTER the Displacement (P.A.D.) of the chess pieces for Equation 30.

30.   O.B. (I w(B (alpha) B/Kn 3H)   - I w(B (beta) C/Kn (alpha prime) 5) ;
            L.T.(1)   T.C.(1)   L.T.(1)   B.R.(0)
; II b(Kn 7H) X I w(Kn (alpha prime) 5 / II b(P 7B - P 5B)).
   T.C.(1)   B.R.(0)   B.C.(0)   B.C.(0)

In Equation 30,part 1,Sections(A/B),for Section(A),Player I Orange-Blue color band White Bishop that previously positioned at Row(alpha),Column(B),Lower Top(L.T.) section, Base(1),uses the Direct Physical single space diagonal movement to displace to Row(beta),Column(C),Lower Top(L.T.) section, Base(1) AND for Section(B), Player I White Knight that previously positioned at Row(3),Column(H),Top Center (T.C.) Platform, Base(1),uses the Direct Abstract 3/2 movement to displace to Row (alpha prime),Column(5),Bottom Right(B.R.) section, Base(0).

LOGIC : In Equation 30,part 1,Section(B),Player I Orange-Blue color band White Knight that positions at Row(alpha prime),Column(5),Bottom Right(B.R.) section, Base(0),now poises an imminent Direct Abstract 3/2 squares THREAT to Player II Black Knight that stations at Row(7),Column(H),Top Center(T.C.) Platform, Base(1).

In Equation 30,part 2,Sections(C/D),for Section(C),Player II Orange-Blue color band Black Knight that previously stationed at Row(7),Column(H),Top Center(T.C.) Platform, Base(1),uses the Direct Abstract 3/2 squares attack movement to capture Player I White Knight that previously positioned at Row(alpha prime),Column(5), Bottom Right(B.R.) section, Base(0) AND for Section(D),Player II Black Pawn that previously stationed at Row(7),Column(B),Bottom Center(B.C.) Platform, Base(0), uses the Direct Physical two spaces <u>vertical</u> (Chess Set # 1, the First Group of letters having a (G-G) initial position configuration) movement to displace to Row(5), Column(B),Bottom Center(B.C.) Platform, Base(0).

Folder 21 / # 8894 – Displays the Position BEFORE the Displacement (P.B.D.) of the chess pieces for Equation 31.

31. O.B. (I w(B (beta) C)   X   II b(Kn (alpha prime) 5 - I w(B (alpha prime) 5 ;
           L.T.(1)   B.R.(0)   T.R.(1)
; II b(P 7G - P 6G)   /   II b(B (beta) D)   X   I w(B(alpha prime) 5)).
  T.C.(1)   T.C.(1)   U.B.(0)   T.R.(1)

Folder 21/ # 8895 – Exhibits the Position AFTER the Displacement (P.A.D.) of the chess pieces for Equation 31.

31. O.B. (I w(B (beta) C) X   II b(Kn (alpha prime) 5) - I w(B (alpha prime) 5 ;
           L.T.(1)   B.R.(0)   T.R.(1)
; II b(P 7G - P 6G) / II b(B (beta) D) X I w(B (alpha prime) 5)).
  T.C.(1)   T.C.(1)   U.B.(0)   T.R.(1)

In Equation 31,part 1,Section(A),Player I Orange-Blue color band White Bishop that previously positioned at Row(beta),Column(C),*Lower Top(L.T.) section, Base(1), uses the *Direct Abstract diagonal attack movement to capture Player II Black Knight that previously stationed at Row(alpha prime),Column(5),*Bottom Right (B.R.) section, Base(0),and LANDING at the INDIRECT coordinate of Row (alpha prime),Column(5),*Top Right(T.R.) section, Base(1).

In Equation 31,part 2,Sections(C/D),for Section(C),Player II Orange-Blue color band Black Pawn that previously stationed at Row(7),Column(G),Top Center(T.C.) Platform, Base(1),uses the Direct Physical single space <u>vertical</u> (Chess Set # 1,the First Group of letters having a (G-G) initial position configuration) movement to displace to Row(6),Column(G),Top Center(T.C.) Platform, Base(1) AND for Section (D),Player II Black Bishop that previously stationed at Row(beta),Column(D), *Upper Bottom(U.B.) section, Base(0),uses the *Direct Abstract diagonal attack movement to capture Player I White Bishop that previously positioned at Row(alpha prime), Column(5),*Top Right(T.R.) section, Base(1).

Folder 21 / # 8896 – Presents the Position BEFORE the Displacement (P.B.D.) of the chess pieces for Equation 32.

32. O.B. (I w(Kn 4A/Q (gamma) F) - I w(Kn (alpha prime) 7/Q (alpha) D) ;
        T.C.(1)   L.B.(0)   B.L.(0)   L.B.(0)
; II b(Kn 6C)   X   I w(Kn (alpha prime) 7)   /   II b(P 5B)   X   I w(P 4C)).
     T.C.(1)   B.L.(0)   B.C.(0)   T.C.(1)

Folder 21 / # 8897 – Reveals the Position AFTER the Displacement (P.A.D.) of the chess pieces for Equation 32.

32.   O.B. (I w(Kn 4A/Q (gamma) F) - I w(Kn (alpha prime) 7/Q (alpha) D ;
               T.C.(1)   L.B.(0)   B.L.(0)   L.B.(0)
; II b(Kn 6C) X I w(Kn (alpha prime) 7) / II b(P 5B) X I w(P 4C)).
     T.C.(1)   B.L.(0)   B.C.(0)   T.C.(1)

In Equation 32,part 1,Sections(A/B),for Section(A),Player I Orange-Blue color band White Knight that previously positioned at Row(4),Column(A),*Top Center(T.C.) Platform, Base(1),uses the *Direct Abstract 4/2 squares movement to displace to Row(alpha prime),Column(7),*Bottom Left(B.L.) section, Base(0) AND for Section (B),Player I White Queen that previously positioned at Row(gamma),Column(F), Lower Bottom(L.B.) section, Base(0),uses the Direct Physical diagonal movement to displace to Row(alpha),Column(D),Lower Bottom(L.B.) section, Base(0).

In Equation 32,part 2,Sections(C/D),for Section(C),Player II Orange-Blue color band Black Knight that previously stationed at Row(6),Column(C),Top Center(T.C.) Platform, Base(1),uses the Direct Abstract 4/2 squares attack movement to capture Player I White Knight that previously positioned at Row(alpha prime),Column(7), Bottom Left(B.L.) section, Base(0) AND for Section(D),Player II Black Pawn that previously stationed at Row(5),Column(B),Bottom Center(B.C.) Platform, Base(0), uses the Direct Abstract single space diagonal attack movement to capture Player I White Pawn that previously positioned at Row(4),Column(C),Top Center(T.C.) Platform, Base(1).

Folder 21 / # 8898 – Illustrates the Position BEFORE the Displacement (P.B.D.) of the chess pieces for Equation 33.

33. O.B. (I w(Q (alpha) D   X   II b(B (alpha prime) 5   ;
                  L.B.(0)   T.R.(1)
  ; II b(Kn (alpha prime) 7 - Kn (beta prime) 4)).
          B.L.(0)   B.L.(0)

Folder 21 / # 8899 – Discloses the Position AFTER the Displacement (P.A.D.) of the chess pieces for Equation 33.

33. O.B. (I w(Q (alpha) D X   II b(B (alpha prime) 5 ;
              L.B.(0)   T.R.(1)
; II b(Kn (alpha prime) 7   - Kn (beta prime) 4)   ).
     B.L.(0)   B.L.(0)

In Equation 33,part 1,Player I Orange-Blue color band White Queen that previously positioned at Row(alpha),Column(D),*Lower Bottom(L.B.) section, Base(0),uses the *Direct Abstract diagonal attack movement to capture Player II Black Bishop that previously stationed at Row(alpha prime),Column(5),*Top Right(T.R.) section, Base (1).

In Equation 33,part 2,Player II Orange-Blue color band Black Knight that previously stationed at Row(alpha prime),Column(7),Bottom Left(B.L.) section, Base(0),uses the Direct Physical 4/2 squares movement to displace to Row(beta prime),Column (4),Bottom Left(B.L.) section, Base(0).

Folder 21 / # 8900 – Explains the Position BEFORE the Displacement (P.B.D.) of the chess pieces for Equation 34.

34. O.B. (I w(Player I forfeits the turn to play) ; II b(P 7F - P 6F)).
T.C.(1)   T.C.(1)

Folder 21 / # 8901 - Illustrates the Position AFTER the Displacement (P.A.D.) of the chess pieces for Equation 34.

34.   O.B. (I w(Player I forfeits the turn to play) ; II b(P 7F - P 6F)).
                                           T.C.(1)   T.C.(1)

In Equation 34,part 1,Player I forfeits the turn to play; Player I does not move any chess pieces.

In Equation 34,part 2,Player II Orange-Blue color band Black Pawn that previously stationed at Row(7),Column(F),Top Center(T.C.) Platform, Base(1),uses the Direct Physical single space <u>vertical</u> movement to displace to Row(6),Column(F),Top Center(T.C.) Platform, Base(1).

Folder 21 / # 8902 – Presents the Position BEFORE the Displacement (P.B.D.) of the chess pieces for Equation 35.

35. O.B.   (I w(Q (alpha prime) 5)   X   II b(Ki (gamma) C ;   ………………
                    T.R.(1)   U.B.(0)   [END] 4.

Folder 21 / # 8903 – Displays the Position AFTER the [CHECKMATE] Capture of Player II Orange-Blue color band Black King that previously stationed at Row (gamma),Column(C), Upper Bottom(U.B.) section, Base(0),by Player I White Queen that previously positioned at Row(alpha prime),Column(5),Top Right(T.R.) section, Base(1).   Player I wins the Orange-Blue color band set. [END] 4. The match ends.

Player I leads the match with a 3-1 victory over Player II.

Folder 21 / # 8904 – Depicts a Close-up view of Equation 35. Player I White Queen captured Player I Black King. Player I wins the Orange-Blue color band set and leads the match with a 3-1 victory over Player II. The match ends. [END] 4.

CLOSING

I thank you for the sponsorship of this book, with the intent of advancing the evolution of Advance 3-D Matrix Vector Logistics Chess. My chess books, (please see: www.amazon.com/author/siafabneal) offer value to the gaming experiences and impressions of chess and allow readers to uniquely experience the pseudo-dynamic and quasi-kinetic World of Advanced 3-d Model Matrix Chess. Do allow yourself to meet the challenge of exploring and of exhausting the tapestry of these intense psychological war games, at any time, if you may.

****

Advance Chess- Model III- The Synergistics Informatics of The Quadruple Set Game, Book 4 Vol. 1 Game # 1, (Q 4.1. G1), (G-G)/(G-G)/(A-A)/(A-A)- by Siafa B. Neal is book twenty-three in his line of professional chess instruction books.

Learn Advance Chess from a Grand master as Siafa who uses diagrams, drawings, illustrations, and photos displaying key information about the game board. Included in this book are detailed descriptions and equations that take readers from the ordinary mundane play of conventional chess to the extraordinary appeal experiences of Advance Chess.

The gamer needs to understand the fundamental aspects of conventional chess to digest and enjoy these expert chess instruction books. Whether you are a Beginner, Intermediate, Semi-Professional or Professional you will enjoy the concepts in this new, exciting Advance Chess instruction book.

If you are a gamer who is bored with conventional chess and are ready to learn and experience the complexities and challenges of intense psychological warfare, this book is for you. If you are a chess player advocate, this exciting new concept will help you acquire gaming knowledge about Advance Chess and allow you to progress ahead of the learning curve well above the Masters and the Grand-Masters of the classical games of conventional chess.

I invite you to enter the pseudo-dynamics and quasi-kinetics World of Chess to explore and to exhaust the opportunities of evaluating the plasticity boundary limit ranges of your full spectrum cognitive elasticity cognition capabilities and potentialities. By doing so, a reader gains a unique perspective about their intelligence levels for Logistics Diagnostics and Prognostics Analysis.

The language of chess is indeed an expression of mathematical spatial relativity and a Universal language.

My Advanced 3-D Model chess books allow readers to tap into the endless potential of Matrix Chess with the hope that the sport of chess gains recognition as an Olympic Sport whereby both humans and robots interact and compete. The possibility exits where Advance 3-D Chess may a recreational activity for the Martian habitants as man reaches further into space and inhabits other planets.

EC Publishing, LLC Endorses the book: Advance Chess -Model III – The Synergistics Informatics of the Quadruple Set Game, Book 4 Vol. 1 Game # 1, (G-G)/(G-G)/(A-A)/(A-A), Subtitled – The Quadruple Set Game -by Siafa B. Neal as the ultimate battle plan in war games. Reviewed on October 30, 2020. Please visit for more information: (https://www.diversecontentliterary.com).

FOOTNOTES

1. Byrne Robert, 'CHESS', the New York Times, January 14, 1997, Accessed

2. Wikipedia, the Free Encyclopedia, Accessed December 20, 2010.

3. World Chess Championship 2014 – Official site (http://www.shochi2014.fide.com). Retrieved 28, May 2015 at 10:39 P.M.

4. Chess tournament, Wikipedia, the Free Encyclopedia, (http://en.wikipedia.org/wiki/chess_tournament).

5. Ibid

6. Hooper, David Whyld, Kenneth (1992). "The Oxford companion to Chess" (second ed.) Oxford University Press.p.426 .ISBN 0-19-866164-9.

7. (http://www.chesshistory.com/winter/winter52.html #5865 note 5869).

8. (http://www.chesshistory.com/winter # 5870 note 5874).

9. Eales, Richard (2002) [1985]. Chess,The History of a Game. , Harding Simpole. ISBN 0-9513757-3-3.

10. Hooper; Whyld, "The Oxford companion to Chess "

11. Fine, Reuben (1983). "The World's Great Chess Games" (second ed.), Dover Publications.pp.14-15 ISBN 0-486-24512-8.

12. Sunnucks, Anne (1970)., The Encyclopedia of Chess, Hale.,ISBN 0-7091-1030-8.

13. Hooper; Whyld, "The Oxford Companion to Chess"

14. Litmanowiez, Wladyslaw & Gizyeki, Jesrzy (1986), Szachy od A do Z, Wydaunictuo, Sport i Turystyka, Warszewa. ISBN 83-217-2481-7.

15. Brace, Edward R. (1977). An Illustrated Dictionary of Chess., Hamlyn Publishing Group p.64. ISBN 1-55521-394-4.

16. FIDE History (http://www.webcitation.org/query?url=http://www.geocities.com/siliconvalley/lab/7578/fide.htm&date=2009-10-25+09:50:00) by Bill Wall. Retrieved 2 November 2008.

17. Brace, "An Illustrated Dictionary of Chess"

18. A History of Chess (http://www.chess-poster.com/english/chesmayne/history_of_chess.htm).

19. Brace, "An Illustrated Dictionary of Chess".

20. Latson, Jennifer. Time magazine, "Did Deep Blue Beat Kasparov Because of a System Glitch", February 17, 2015, (http://time.com/3705316/deep-blue-kasparov).

21. Kasparov,Gary. Time magazine, "The Day I sensed a new Kind of Intelligence", (Monday, March 25,1996). Retrieved on 07/25/15 at 9:45 P.M. (http://content.time.com/time/subscriber/article /0,33009,984305-1,00.html).

22. Ibid. (paras: 1,2 (retrieved on 07/25/15 at 10:45 P.M.), 3 (retrieved on 07/25/15 at 10:55 P.M.) , 4 (retrieved on 07/25/15 at 11:15 P.M.) , 5 (retrieved on 07/25/15 at 11:30 P.M.) , 6 (retrieved on 07/25/15 at 11:45 P.M.), 7 (retrieved on 07/26/15 at 12:01 A.M.).

23. Latson, Time, "Did Deep Blue Beat…." / see (Footnote 1, para.3). Retrieved on 07/25/15 at 2:15 P.M. (Added notation on 07/26/15 at 12:42 A.M.).

24. Ibid. (para.6). Notation date 07/26/15 at 1:01 A.M.).

25. Ibid. NPR (Public News station) (para.6 Retrieved on 07/25/15 at 2:15 P.M.) Notation added 07/26/15 at 1:33 A.M.

26. Ibid. Wired. (para7).

27. Greenblatt, Richard D., Eastlake Donald E. III, and Crocker, Stephen D. (1 April 1969), retrieved on 07/26/15. "The Greenblatt Chess Program (AIM-174)" (http://hdl.handle.net/1721.1/6176). Massachusetts Institute of Technology. Retrieved 2006-12-27.

28. Results of the WMCCC and WCCC from the ICGA (http://www.grappa.univ-lille 3 .fr/icga/game.php?id=1). Retrieved November 9,2008.

29. E.R. INK (1983). Шахmamбl u mamemamuka, (http://ilib.mirror 1.mccme.ru/djvu/bib-kvant/chess.htm)., Hayka, Mockla. (in Russian).

30. Wikipedia, The free encyclopedia, "Chess tournament", (http://en.wikipedia.org/wiki/chess_tournament).

31. Silver, Alexander, Time magazine, "Gary Kasparov vs. Deep Blue", Tuesday, February 15, 2011, Retrieved on 07/25/2015 at 3:15 P.M., updated on 11/30/15 at 11:26 P.M.

32. Ibid.

33. Kasparov, Gary, (Monday, May 26,1997), "IBM owes Mankind a Rematch," (a Time exclusive: Still smarting from his stunning defeat, Gary Kasparov back to the Computer that defeats him), (http://content.time.com/time/subscriber/article/0330009,986394,00.html).

34. Haire, Meaghan. Time magazine, "Should Chess be an Olympic Sport?". (Tuesday, August 05,2008) (paras. :1,2) Retrieved on 09/27/2015 at 3:35 P.M. (http://content.time/world/article/0,8599,1827716,000.html). Added notation on 09/27/15 at 10:30 P.M.

35. Ibid. (paras.: 3,4). Retrieved on 09/27/15 at 3:35 P.M. Added notation on 09/27/15 at 11:15 P.M.

36. Ibid. (para. 5). Retrieved on 09/27/2015 at 3:35 P.M. Added notations on 09/27/15 at 11:56 P.M.

37. Ibid. (para.6).

38. Ibid. (para. 7).

39. Ibid. (paras.: 9,10)

40. Christophi, Helen, The Courthouse News, "Chess Champion Touts Benefits of AI, Downplays Fears", May 10,2018 (https://www.courthousenews.com/chess-champion-touts -benefits-of-ai-downplays-fear/) , retrieved on 05/11/18 at 9:35 P.M.

****